MOUNTAIN
WORLDS

National
Geographic
Society

MOUNTAIN
WORLDS

MOUNTAIN WORLDS

Published by
The National Geographic
Society

Gilbert M. Grosvenor
*President and
Chairman of the Board*

Owen R. Anderson
Executive Vice President

Robert L. Breeden
*Senior Vice President,
Publications and
Educational Media*

Prepared by
National Geographic
Book Service

Charles O. Hyman
Director

Ross S. Bennett
Associate Director

Margaret Sedeen
Managing Editor

Susan C. Eckert
Director of Research

Staff for this book

Margaret Sedeen
Editor

Linda B. Meyerriecks
Illustrations Editor

David M. Seager
Art Director

Catherine Herbert Howell
Chief Researcher

Mary B. Dickinson
Edward Lanouette
Carol Bittig Lutyk
Elizabeth L. Newhouse
Robert M. Poole
David F. Robinson
Shirley L. Scott
Jonathan B. Tourtellot
Editor-Writers

Ratri Banerjee
Gretchen C. Bordelon
Cathryn P. Buchanan
Paulette L. Claus
Suzanne Kane Poole
Lise Swinson Sajewski
Jean Kaplan Teichroew
Anne E. Withers
Editorial Researchers

Paulette L. Claus
Map Coordinator

Anne E. Withers
Style

Barry C. Bishop
Vice Chairman, Committee
for Research and Exploration,
National Geographic Society
and
Melvin G. Marcus,
Professor of Geography,
Arizona State University
Chief Consultants

Greta Arnold
Illustrations Researcher

Michael Frost
D. Samantha Johnston
Diana E. McFadden
Illustrations Assistants

Karen F. Edwards
Traffic Manager

Chapter Maps by
John D. Garst, Jr.
Judith F. Bell
Peter J. Balch
D. Mark Carlson

Donald L. Carrick
Robert W. Cronan
Marguerite Suarez Dunn
Hildegard B. Groves
Gary M. Johnson
Joseph F. Ochlak
Daniel J. Ortiz
Isaac Ortiz
Nancy S. Stanford
Kevin Q. Stuebe
Barbara L. Trapido
Martin S. Walz
Publications Art

David L. Aagesen
Jean B. Berthold
Geography Interns

Charlotte Golin
Design Assistant

John T. Dunn
Technical Director

Richard S. Wain
Production Manager

Andrea Crosman
Production Coordinator

Leslie A. Adams
Production Assistant

David V. Evans
Quality Control Manager

Teresita Cóquia Sison
Editorial Assistant

Stephany J. Freedman
Indexer

R. Gary Colbert
Administrative Assistant

Louisa Clayton
Sallie M. Greenwood
Stuart McCutchan
Robert W. Northrop
Melanie Patt-Corner
Maura J. Pollin
Jane Alexandra Walsh
Contributors

Moonrise over Mount Brooks,
Denali National Park and Preserve,
Alaska.
By Rick McIntyre

First edition: 153,000
320 pages, 315 illustrations,
including
296 photographs and 19 maps.

CONTENTS

LOOK TO THE MOUNTAINS

William E. Thompson

One upward glance, and it was there. The highest, most perfect peak in the universe.

The next moment it was gone. No cataclysm, no noise. It simply vanished, and with it all the other bulges, eruptions, and folds on Earth's surface that we call mountains. They all disappeared, blown traceless onto a wrinkle-free, monotonous globe.

I jerked awake to peer over the cocoon of the sleeping bag. There, soaring 3,000 feet above me, the brutish, icy peak still loomed in the dark, just as huge and real and wondrous as it had seemed before I'd fallen asleep.

It was a long-ago teenager's fitful dream during a night on a rock ledge in the Cascades. But I have often mused over the fantasy. What would be lost had the dream been real? What is the meaning of these things we call mountains? How does their presence affect the human experience?

Mountains. They span the globe, swell the oceans, and rise on all continents and major islands. They are the Sierra Nevada, Cascades, Coast Ranges, Alaska and Brooks Ranges, the Appalachians—and the Rockies, with more than a hundred different ranges large enough to have their own names. They are the peaks of the Antarctic, and the Andes and the Sierra Madres. They are island mountains like Tahiti, Hawaii, and the Azores, and mountainous islands like New Zealand and Greenland. They are the Hima-

Aerial view of the Himalayan lower ranges from the Khumbu region, Nepal.

layas, buttressing the thousand-mile-wide Tibetan Plateau that averages 15,000 feet—higher than anything in the contiguous United States. They are the Atlas and Kilimanjaro and Kenya. They are the Pyrenees, Caucasus, the Alps that dominate western Europe, and the Urals, the traditional boundary between Europe and Asia.

Their names sing of wild places and unfenced spaces—Ruwenzori, Tetons, Hindu Kush, Dolomites, Uinta, Sangre de Cristo, Bitterroot, Allegheny, Gallatin, Karakorams. Mountains command the eye and enlarge the being. They dominate the globe like no other natural thing except the oceans.

But what is a mountain? Scholars have yet to agree. Some say a landmass must reach at least 3,000 feet and have "conspicuity." This disqualifies the Pennines of Britain and parts of the Appalachians. In fact, some geographers dismiss most of those chains as "hill country." Not so, say others. "Ignore altitude; pay attention to the geologic structure." Given that, the folded, metamorphic bedrock of New York's Central Park would qualify, where outcroppings that lie exposed today are the eroded stumps of mountains that arose beginning almost half a billion years ago.

An eloquent description was that of British mountaineer Geoffrey Winthrop Young: "Earth set on earth a little higher." Young's mountain is comparative. And personal—whatever strikes fire in the imagination. One person's mountain, another person's knoll.

Everything from the wrath of God to volcanic eruption has been cited to explain the origin of mountains. Until late in the 17th century, wind escaping from Earth's interior was thought to inflate mountains, like great, pocked balloons. Mountains were also thought to be Earth bones, growing like human bones, in a layer of Earth skin. Edmund Halley's study of comets led him, by 1694, to claim that the shock of Earth's passing through a comet tail caused the biblical Flood and much attendant violence, such as the "heaping up" of mountains and, by a kind of wave action, ranges as well.

In Africa's Great Rift Valley, fossil finds have pushed the emergence of human ancestors to some 3.6 million years ago. That figure is nothing when set against the age of some of Earth's peaks. True, some ranges are infants. The Himalayan uplift began only some 50 million years ago, and the present Alps perhaps as little as 3 million years ago. When did the first granitelike peak rise on Earth? No one can say. The first 700 million years of Earth history have been obliterated.

Most scientists agree on the theory of global plate tectonics, that the continents and ocean basins ride around on crustal plates, earthquakes rumbling out from where the plates pull apart or grind against each other.

Oceanic plates are created from molten rock which wells up beneath the world's greatest mountain range, the Mid-Ocean Ridge. Over 46,000 miles long, this submarine network of mountain chains envelops nearly as much area as all the continents combined. It has peaks that rise 13,000 feet above the ocean floor. A rift splits its spine, some places thousands of feet deep. From this central valley flows the molten rock that creates the plates. The plates move away from each other, the new crust cooling and contracting as they go.

When plates collide, the thin skin of Earth is thrust up, creating mountains from the wreckage. Where a dense oceanic plate bends down under a continent, as an East Pacific plate does under South America, volcanoes fuel the mountains that arch up at the edge of the continental plate. The Andes were made this way, and the Cascades.

When continent meets continent the contest is even more titanic, as neither plate can easily descend into the denser layers of the deep Earth. India resists, but it is inexorably driven under the southern flank of Asia, doubling the thickness of the crust and piling up the Himalayas and the Tibetan Plateau on its northward push. The Himalayas rise about an inch every five years. These mountains are called folded.

For at least the last billion years, plates

have jockeyed for position on the finite globe. The Appalachians are the remnants of the collisions some 300 to 400 million years ago of North America against Europe and then Africa. The heat and pressure of these collisions raised and folded mountains of perhaps Alpine stature in several resurgent pulses.

When this amalgamation of continents tore apart, starting about 200 million years ago, it did so piecemeal. Africa tugged free and drifted eastward, followed by Europe, opening the present Atlantic Ocean. Caught between the continents was a variety of smaller chunks. One of these microplates carries the Italian peninsula, which is being shoved into the belly of Europe by the northward pinch of Africa, pressing up the Alpine wall in a sweep of peaks that rises about half an inch every ten years.

Just as plate collision shoves upward, a quietly pervasive force—gravity—pulls down again. Its visible agents are rain, the streams, the wind, the glaciers that carve and gouge— the movers that eventually expose the bones of every range.

Tramping in his beloved Yosemite, John Muir examined the canyons of the High Sierra, and rightfully attributed their shape to the work of glaciers. Though sun warmed the lakes and meadows that stretched before him, Muir's imagination set the ice creeping southward again. "The last days of this glacial winter are not yet past; we live in 'creation's dawn'," Muir wrote in 1873. "The world, though made, is still being made and becoming more beautiful every day."

Mountains have played many different roles in human life. They have been pathway to heaven and home of the gods, sacred to religions of all eras. Moses climbed Mount Sinai for the Ten Commandments, Olympus was home for the Greek gods, Kikuyu worship N'Gai on Mount Kenya, the ark landed on Mount Ararat in Turkey, Muhammad saw the angel Gabriel on Mount Hira, Inca altars stood on Andean summits, St. Patrick prayed atop Croagh Patrick, and Tibet's Mount Kailas is a focus for both Hindus and Buddhists.

Mountains can be barriers, but passes can be windows to emigration, conquest, and trade, conduits for the movement of peoples and ideas, or havens for refugees. There were daring marches across high Alpine passes by Attila, Napoléon, and, of course, Hannibal with his 37 bewildered elephants and 46,000 freezing troops. Consider the vision, in another time and place, of a westering American family as it searched for an opening in the sheer, snow-swathed Sierran wall barring the way to the rich life beyond.

Like rivers, mountain crests serve as boundaries in many places. The Pyrenees divide France and Spain; the Andes stand between Chile and Argentina. In 1973 I saw the effects of a mountaintop boundary when I was on a climbing trip with Barry Bishop. Ten years earlier Barry had carried the National Geographic Society's flag to the summit of 29,028-foot Mount Everest on the first American ascent of the Himalayan peak. In the Ötztal Alps Barry and I traversed a craggy mountain crest that defined the Austrian-Italian border, a phenomenon with more tension than the climbing itself.

War has bent and shifted boundaries throughout Europe. After World War I, the Austrian loss of the South Tirol meant cession of over 300,000 German-speaking inhabitants to Italy. Many unfortunate cultural changes followed the arbitrary establishment of the border along the mountain crest. The German-speaking people had to recognize Italian as their official language. Under Mussolini, everything with German inscriptions was obliterated, including gravestones. A generation later warnings in an Austrian guide for climbers echoed the old tensions: *Climbers are officially not allowed to cross the border. Climbers should take care and obey the guards, who have been known to shoot at climbers who have ignored warnings.*

In the French Alps, Barry and I talked with an elderly woman who lived on a hardscrabble farm near Little St. Bernard Pass. Life was a fight against ice, poor soil, short growing seasons, and cold. Barry asked her if she

North Pacific Ocean

KOLYMA RANGE

ALASKA

+ Mt. McKinley
20,320 ft

RANGE

Mt. Logan
19,524 ft +

BROOKS RANGE

Arctic Ocean

COAST MOUNTAINS

CASCADE RANGE

SIERRA NEVADA

ROCKY MOUNTAINS

+ Mt. Robson
12,972 ft

North
Pole

+ Barbeau Peak
8,544 ft

60° N

URAL MOUNTAINS

NORTH
AMERICA

+ Mt. Elbert
14,433 ft

SIERRA MADRE

Gunnbjørn
12,139 ft +

ARCTIC CIRCLE

60° N

EUROPE

CAUCASUS
MOUNTAINS

Orizaba
18,855 ft +

APPALACHIAN MOUNTAINS

Mt. Mitchell   Mt. Washington
6,684 ft   6,288 ft

North Atlantic Ocean

CARPATHIAN
MOUNTAINS →

El'brus
18,510 ft

South
Pacific
Ocean

Mt. Blanc + ALPS
15,771 ft

Co. Chirripó +
12,530 ft

PYRENEES

ATLAS MOUNTAINS

30° N

+ Jebel Toubkal
13,665 ft

ANDES

GUIANA HIGHLANDS

AFRICA

Pico da Neblina
9,888 ft +

Co. Ojos del Salado
22,572 ft

SOUTH
AMERICA

Co. Aconcagua
22,834 ft

BRAZILIAN
HIGHLANDS

EQUATOR

+ Cameroon Mt.
13,451 ft

A N D E S

+ Pico da Bandeira
9,482 ft

60° W

30° S

South Atlantic Ocean

150° W

120° W

90° W

30° W

0°

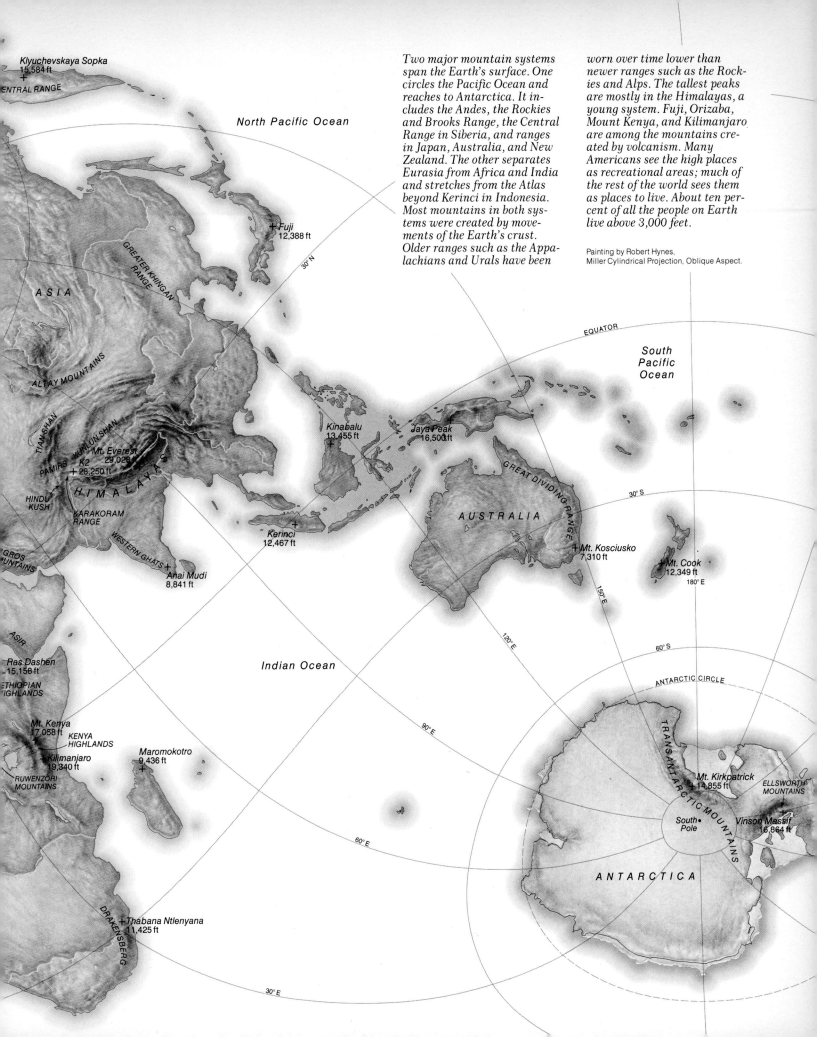

Two major mountain systems span the Earth's surface. One circles the Pacific Ocean and reaches to Antarctica. It includes the Andes, the Rockies and Brooks Range, the Central Range in Siberia, and ranges in Japan, Australia, and New Zealand. The other separates Eurasia from Africa and India and stretches from the Atlas beyond Kerinci in Indonesia. Most mountains in both systems were created by movements of the Earth's crust. Older ranges such as the Appalachians and Urals have been worn over time lower than newer ranges such as the Rockies and Alps. The tallest peaks are mostly in the Himalayas, a young system. Fuji, Orizaba, Mount Kenya, and Kilimanjaro are among the mountains created by volcanism. Many Americans see the high places as recreational areas; much of the rest of the world sees them as places to live. About ten percent of all the people on Earth live above 3,000 feet.

Painting by Robert Hynes,
Miller Cylindrical Projection, Oblique Aspect.

Klyuchevskaya Sopka
15,584 ft

CENTRAL RANGE

North Pacific Ocean

30° N

Fuji
12,388 ft

ASIA

GREATER KHINGAN RANGE

ALTAY MOUNTAINS

TIAN SHAN
KUNLUN SHAN
PAMIRS
K2
28,250 ft
Mt. Everest
29,028 ft
HIMALAYAS

HINDU KUSH

KARAKORAM RANGE

ZAGROS MOUNTAINS

WESTERN GHATS

Anai Mudi
8,841 ft

Kinabalu
13,455 ft

EQUATOR

Jaya Peak
16,500 ft

South Pacific Ocean

GREAT DIVIDING RANGE

AUSTRALIA

Kerinci
12,467 ft

30° S

Mt. Kosciusko
7,310 ft

Mt. Cook
12,349 ft

180° E

150° E

120° E

90° E

60° S

ASIR

Ras Dashen
15,158 ft

ETHIOPIAN HIGHLANDS

Indian Ocean

ANTARCTIC CIRCLE

Mt. Kenya
17,058 ft

KENYA HIGHLANDS

Kilimanjaro
19,340 ft

RUWENZORI MOUNTAINS

Maromokotro
9,436 ft

TRANSANTARCTIC MOUNTAINS

Mt. Kirkpatrick
14,855 ft

ELLSWORTH MOUNTAINS

South Pole

Vinson Massif
16,864 ft

60° E

ANTARCTICA

DRAKENSBERG

Thabana Ntlenyana
11,425 ft

30° E

thought Hannibal might have passed, 2,200 years ago, near where her cottage now stands. The answer was brusque. She really didn't know, but "even if he had, he was quick to head downhill."

Up high, the lowlander's body can be a sick stranger. Nausea, loss of appetite, cruel headaches, pulmonary edema and embolism, and heart failure can afflict even the young and fit lowlander. But the body can acclimatize, and people do live up to about 17,000 feet in Andean valleys and Tibetan heights. Above that altitude the body can endure only a few months without deterioration.

In the 16th century, Spanish soldiers traveled in the Peruvian Andes. With them was a Jesuit, José de Acosta. Crossing a 15,000-foot pass, Father Acosta fell victim to acute altitude sickness. "I was suddenly surprized with so mortall and strange.... pangs of straining and casting as I thought to cast up my soul too; for having cast up meate, fleugme, and choller . . . in the end I cast up blood." Some of Father Acosta's companions begged for confession, thinking they were near death. But the agonies vanished in a few hours, at a lower altitude.

The priest felt he was in one of the world's highest places. "The Pirenees, and the Alpes of Italie, are as ordinarie houses [compared to these] Towers," he wrote, and intuitively assigned the sickness to the low atmospheric pressure that reduces the amount of oxygen in every gulp of air. "The aire is there so subtile and delicate, as it is not proportionable with the breathing of man."

The Quechua Indians of the high Andes, and some other mountain peoples, show physiological adaptations that fascinate and perplex scientists. Their barrel chests give the Quechuas a large lung capacity, enabling them to carry more air in and out than lowlanders can, and to move more oxygen into their blood. Their blood has more red cells, increasing its oxygen-carrying hemoglobin. The Sherpas of Nepal don't have all the same characteristics, yet their ability to work hard at high altitudes is well known.

Life in the mountain world is governed not just by cold and altitude, but by relentless gravity. Whether tugging at terraced fields or slamming avalanches and mudflows through entire towns, gravity takes its toll. Avalanches were a natural hazard of the winter campaigns of World War I. They also became a weapon. Armies fired artillery rounds into snow-laden slopes above the enemy. In one two-day period, when both Austrians and Italians shelled the slopes, snow buried 18,000 soldiers. Tens of thousands of Austrian and Italian troops died in the Dolomites because of avalanches. Today avalanche-control crews protect mountain towns and ski resorts by triggering avalanches with explosives before the snow kicks itself loose.

The Andes have seen some of history's greatest natural disasters. In 1962 a three-million-ton chunk of ice from a glacier on Huascarán, Peru's highest mountain, broke free at about 21,000 feet. It came to rest a few minutes later, nine miles below, killing more than 3,500 people and devastating nine villages. In 1970 an earthquake sent a huge avalanche crashing down from Huascarán at 200 miles an hour. The debris destroyed two villages that lay in its path. The earthquake itself took 70,000 lives and damaged houses a hundred miles from the epicenter.

In Colombia, after a lull of 400 years, the Nevado del Ruiz volcano erupted in 1985, melting snow and glacial ice on the mountain's peak. At 25 miles an hour, a wall of mud, ash, and rocks careened through the valleys, uprooted trees, and leveled houses. When it was finished, 23,000 Colombians were dead.

The mountaineer George Mallory, to the question of why he wanted to risk all in an attempt on Everest, answered, "Because it is there." Others have had different motives—science, adventure, exploration, mapmaking—but one compelling reason is the challenge. That spirit has sent mountaineers tramping into the hills to find themselves and what a climbing friend of mine calls "the creature." To seek the creature because

Pages 14-15: Earth's highest mountain, Everest (left, center), pierces the jet stream at 29,028 feet above sea level. Its summit is marine limestone that formed on the floor of a shallow, tropical sea 300 million years ago.
William E. Thompson

Pages 16-17: Clouds veil the peaks of Huang Shan, a holy mountain in China's Anhui Province. The Chinese believe that ascending such peaks heightens the spirit. Pilgrims have sought inspiration from Huang Shan's granite, mist, and pines for more than a thousand years.
Marc Riboud

Pages 18-19: Terracing and channel irrigation create much of the arable land in the lower Himalayas of Nepal. Landslides like those at lower right are a hazard of these deforested slopes.
William E. Thompson

it's there may be the simplest definition of mountaineering—useless, dangerous, exhilarating, and, perhaps, the grandest consummation of mental, spiritual, and physical effort.

The creature is the same for a solo climber stretched to human limits on Yosemite's El Capitan as it was for Edmund Hillary and Tenzing Norgay, the first to top Everest, as it was on Everest for Barry Bishop, as it was earlier for Alexandra David-Néel when she trekked the high passes of the Tibetan Plateau in 1923 and 1924. The motive had a spiritual essence for Israel C. Russell nearly a century ago when he led the National Geographic Society's first expedition, to map Mount St. Elias in unexplored borderlands between Alaska and Canada. The creature was with Bradford Washburn as he stood on the summit of Mount McKinley in 1951 to complete the survey of the roof of North America, and felt as though he were "looking out the very windows of heaven."

Climbers have achieved all the major peaks. Most problems of elevation, steepness, and distance have been overcome. What remains is style, an assertion of originality and a personal standard of perfection.

And joy remains. As a young man Barry Bishop fulfilled a dream with a solo climb of the Matterhorn's Hörnli Ridge. He saw no one on the ascent, and he stood alone on the summit for nearly an hour before turning away. As he neared the lower slopes, he heard behind him the light whistling of another climber. Barry stopped, curious about the stranger. Soon an older man appeared, with a bouncing gait. He had come across the top, from Italy, a severe route that he took each year on his birthday. The man talked of other mountain worlds he had known, of endurance and discipline, of glorious self-forgetfulness, and of movement into beauty, adventure, and the unknown.

"It was," Barry said later, "as if he felt himself to be newly made."

Mountain scenes nourish us all, and every year draw more and more people to the heights. The pressures on fragile environments can destroy the very beauty we seek. The number of trekkers on the slopes below Everest increased fivefold from 1971 to 1981. Their demands jeopardize ancient patterns of both nature and culture. In the Peruvian Andes more than 100,000 people a year visit Machu Picchu, the 15th-century Inca settlement, leaving behind garbage, vandalized stonework, and polluted streams.

Some places in the United States suffer also. In 1950, 141 climbers struggled to the cratered summit of Washington's Mount Rainier, 14,410 feet above Puget Sound. Now nearly 4,000 people a year reach the top, and another 4,000 attempt it. Each year helicopters remove 3,500 pounds of trash from the two camps at 10,000 feet. Park rangers estimate that people leave six tons on the mountain every year.

Human populations on mountain slopes—in the Andes, Nepal, the Middle East, northern Africa—have permanently changed the face of the land. They have cut what were widespread forests in a search for fuel and cropland more intensive than the rate at which the forests could maintain themselves. Overgrazing, too, has stripped vegetation, leading to erosion of already thin soils.

Now we are learning how to use our mountain worlds as we conserve them. One effort, guided by the International Biosphere Reserve project, an offshoot of UNESCO's Man and the Biosphere Program, tries to preserve the vitality and diversity of natural ecosystems. One MAB approach is to help people strengthen their local economy and end harmful exploitation of natural resources. The program puts an official stamp on what we already know, that we humans are part of these mountains, not beings that walk and climb in them without connection. The conservation measures are not for the mountains. They are for us. They are for what the mountains can teach of life, of balance, of freedom.

By Dennis G. Hanson

Pages 20-21: Cordillera de Paine's harsh winds and vertical walls guard this Patagonian massif against all but the most dedicated climbers. These peaks in southern Chile are so remote that getting there is almost as difficult as the ascent.
George F. Mobley,
National Geographic Photographer

Pages 22-23: Layers of sediment in the cliffs along the Gilgit River in the Hindu Raj Range show how parts of Asia are being lifted and folded by Earth's tectonic movements.
George F. Mobley,
National Geographic Photographer

Pages 24-25: Summer climbers cross a snow-covered ridge before ascending the granite peaks of Mont Blanc, the highest mountain in western Europe and one of the world's most crowded climbing areas.
Paul Chesley

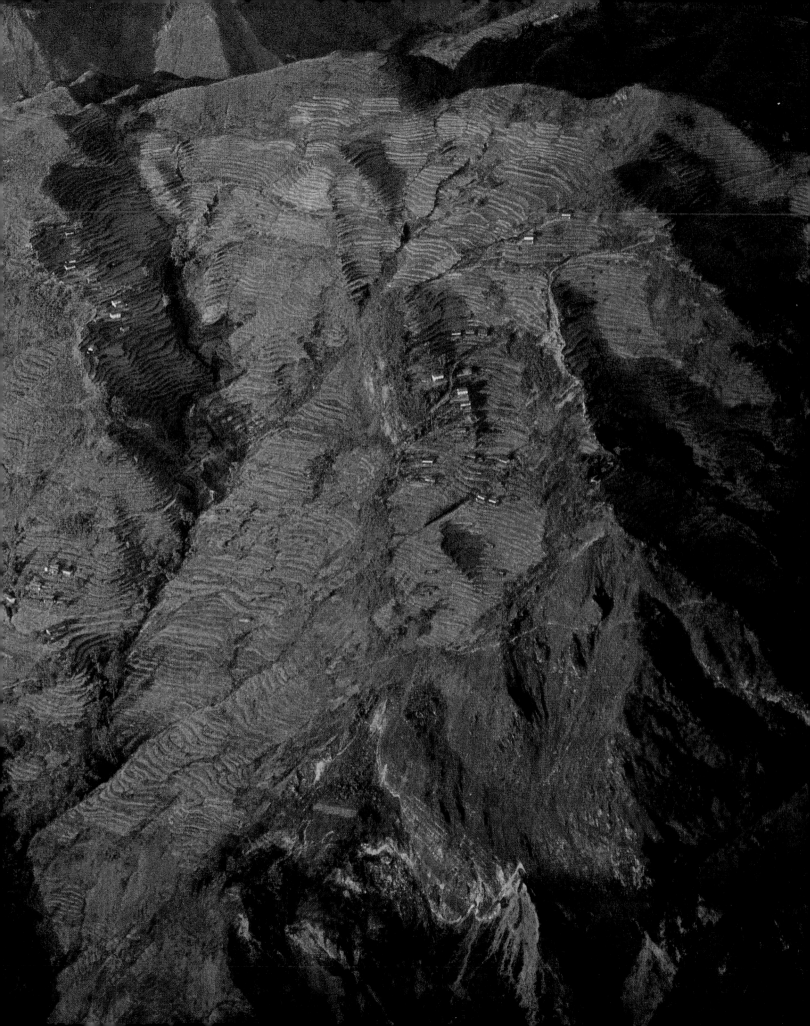

Climbers reach a summit in West Virginia's Seneca Rocks National Recreation Area.

CHANGING WORLDS

Wilderness or development? In West Virginia ecologists and economists attempt to balance the need for more tourist facilities, increased timber and coal production, and more homesites against protection for wildlife, watersheds, and the natural beauty that attracts visitors to the Mountain State.

All over our planet, change comes to once remote mountain worlds, change that affects both human and natural ecology. The needs of an ever growing population must be met—needs of the spirit as well as the body. But what is the greatest value and wisest use of a mountain?

Answers to this now urgent question vary like the peaks themselves. In Switzerland experts assess the impact of tourism on popular sections of the Alps. In the United States the government gave a mountain range back to nature, providing a wild haven for city folk but displacing families who still call the Smokies "home."

Jodi Cobb, National Geographic Photographer

Preserving Europe's Playground

Wood smoke rose from a chalet in a mountain clearing above the village of Château-d'Oex. Bells jangled faintly from the stable, where cows stirred after their early morning milking. Soon a farmer led them out in a plodding procession. As they moved, their bells chimed in ragged sequence, scattering across the valley the echoes of Switzerland's ageless pastoral anthem.

The steep meadows around me on the mountain were buttressed by stone walls, terraced by cows' hooves, shorn by cows' teeth. Down below, chalet homes spread out from the village among pastures and hayfields manicured by grazing and the recent harvest. But wilderness beckoned above the cultivated slopes. Bare-topped crags rimmed the green valley, part of a region called the Pays-d'Enhaut—"high country"—in the low-lying Vaudois Alps.

Many such green basins dot the Alps, the 620-mile-long series of mountain ranges that forms Europe's backbone. Each valley seems to cup a separate mountain world, its farming traditions molded in relative isolation long before the days of railroads and highways. Improved transportation in the 19th and 20th centuries brought first a trickle, then a flood of sightseers and sports enthusiasts, who now help support the Alpine economy. I was curious to see how the influx of tourism had affected these small worlds. Had their rural character and scenic landscape survived?

Sunset's glow warms the icy north face of the Mönch in Switzerland's Bernese Alps.

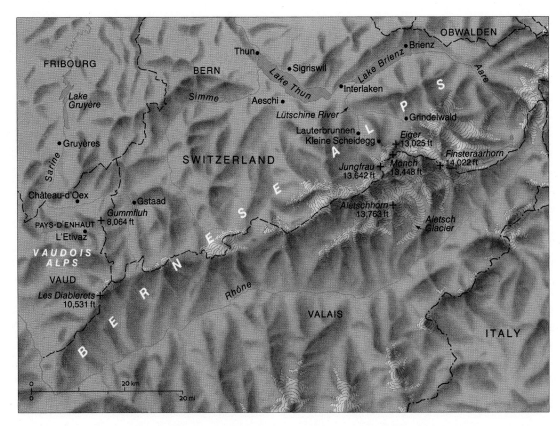

Thrust up from an ancient sea-bed by colliding continental plates, Europe's Alpine region rose and eroded several times. The Alps that arc today from the French Riviera to the Austrian capital of Vienna began growing some 3 million years ago. Many peaks top 10,000 feet, but 1,200 glaciers continue the work of erosion. The largest, Aletsch Glacier, spreads more than 50 square miles over the Bernese Alps.

Switzerland's mountains, whether the towering Bernese Alps or gentler ranges such as the Vaudois Alps, have drawn an increasing number of tourists since the 19th century. Tourist development now threatens the beauty of many such Alpine playgrounds.

The Swiss government asked these same questions in the late 1970s through studies made under the international Man and the Biosphere (MAB) Program. The focus of the studies—the impact of humans on mountain ecosystems—made clear the government's growing unease over heedless tourist development. Tourists expect to find country in the countryside. "First the cows leave, then the guests—who should we milk now?" runs one catchphrase. Mountain farmers assume the role of "landscape gardeners" protecting the nation's rural heritage. Landscape is the raw material—the capital—of tourism. Don't touch the capital!

In the Pays-d'Enhaut, claims former MAB researcher Erwin Stucki, the capital remains intact. Dedicated to work at the grass-roots level, Stucki has moved his young family to Château-d'Oex to be close to his two jobs: He

devotes half his time to directing a new research center that studies rural issues and the mountain environment and the remainder to acting as regional advisor to the Pays-d'Enhaut Development Association.

Six or seven years ago, he told me, the MAB scientists came here expecting to study an ecological problem, much as they were doing at other test areas such as Grindelwald: Had tourist development supplanted traditional farm life? Had ski runs and cable cars destroyed forests and pastures? It turned out, he said, that the local community had maintained an enviable balance between tourism, agriculture, and the environment. Nobody's quite sure how. Part of the reason may be that the proportion of farmers—who bring a conservative vote to land development issues—is high at 23 percent. In Grindelwald, by comparison, it is only about 10 percent.

In Château-d'Oex crane arms swing over chalet-style vacation homes under construction; careful local regulations govern both building styles and zones. New homeowners are just as eager as older ones to preserve the friendly village atmosphere, the slow pace, the traditional rhythm of the changing seasons. In the fall, hay carts scatter wisps of straw along Château-d'Oex's main street, and, at unpredictable intervals but as surely as the leaves turn, the farmers bring their cows down from the mountain pastures.

Practiced ears catch the distinctive clang of bells in the distance, and people race outside. The sound swells to a deafening clamor as the parade draws near. Along the road stride farmers and their sons in short-sleeved black velvet jackets; women and girls march with them, some in blue jeans, others in velvet bodices and striped aprons. And between them file the brown-and-white queens of the pasture, crowned with evergreens and flowers, their huge bells tolling in triumph. Residents toast them from windows along the route. Cars and trucks creep along behind, their drivers grinning broadly. The cows' milk supply, stimulated by calf bearing in the spring, is now slowing down, and the cheese harvest is over. It's time to celebrate.

More than 60 farmers make cheese by hand in the mountains of the Pays-d'Enhaut. The cheese-making chalets, about two-thirds of them privately owned and the others the property of the community, stand on pastureland known locally as *alpages*—alps. The farmers drive their cows up from valley farms onto the mountain in spring, where they graze them part of the time on mid-level alps, and part on higher ones above the tree line. Some of the cows *(Continued on page 37)*

(Continued on page 37)

Decked like dowagers at a garden party, Château-d'Oex milkers return in fall from mountain pastures. The annual descent, known as désalpe *in the French-speaking canton of Vaud, becomes* Alpabfahrt *in German-speaking Bern.*

Pages 32-33: Look-alike green mountain valleys with dark stands of spruce or pine dot the Alps. This one lies east of Gruyères. Others abound in the Pays-d'Enhaut, the Bernese Alps, and in Austria and Italy.

Pages 34-35: Twin windows frame the inhabitants of a Château-d'Oex granary built "by the grace of God" in 1732. Many old Swiss chalets bear similar pious inscriptions.

"Mountain cheese has more flavor than cheese made in the lowlands," says John Zulauf. Clad in an apron, he lifts hot curds from a cheese kettle with his brother. "The grass is of better quality, and there are plenty of flowers." Old cream scoops used for tasting hang on their chalet wall. The steaming curds, dumped into a mold, set in a few minutes. A neighboring farmer places his freshly made cheese wheel in a wooden press. There it will drain for a day or two before he sends it down to the valley.

Cheeses ripen for up to three years at the cooperative cheese cellar (left) in nearby l'Etivaz. "You can find it by the smell," says a local wag. Its racks hold 7,500 cheeses; annexes raise the total storage capacity to 13,000. All cheese made in the area is of the firm, pale yellow Gruyère type, with a nutty flavor and few holes.

belong to them, others they rent for a percentage of the cheese profit. In midsummer the cows descend to the mid-level alps. Here they stay until the threat of snow forces them back down to their valley homes in the fall.

One morning I climbed to a low alp on "the tooth"—La Dent Mountain—to watch John Zulauf make his 212th cheese of the season. With the measured gestures of 30 years' experience, Zulauf poured milk into a copper kettle, then swiveled it over the fire. He added rennet to curdle the milk and sliced through the curds with a cheese harp. Stirring followed, and more heating, and tasting. At the critical moment, Zulauf and a helper swooped a cheesecloth down through the liquid and heaved the dripping bundle of curds into a circular mold. The whey ran down the counter into a tub where leftover bread floated in yesterday's whey. During a lull, Zulauf carried buckets of this swill to troughs outside and released from their sties a tumbling, grunting, squealing pink tangle of pigs. "Whey makes the best pork," he said.

In the valleys of the Pays-d'Enhaut, tall stacks of planks in sawmill yards testify to another major source of income besides dairy farming: forestry. And Erwin Stucki, who encourages Château-d'Oex youngsters to take part in local affairs, talks about the growing number of students signing up for carpentry, masonry, and agriculture schools. Young people have been leaving the village due to lack of jobs. "Now they see more of a future here than they did 15 years ago," said Stucki.

Tourism provides work for many people. Charles-André Ramseier, Château-d'Oex's tall, boyish-looking tourist director, coordinates activities such as skiing, fishing, hiking, and, his pet project, an international hot-air balloon competition each January. Château-d'Oex is a family resort, Ramseier told me, and many people return regularly. But even at peak season, the local life holds its own. The population of about 3,000 almost balances the number of visitors.

On a hot September afternoon, Château-d'Oex wears the air of a sleepy market town

rather than a flourishing mountain resort, but the main street reveals its dual nature. At one end the shell of a new sports center for residents and tourists rises near tennis courts and a miniature golf course. At the other, the sound of a steel hammer rings from a foundry where a smith shapes copper kettles. And on a house wall at the corner of a steep road where the cows come down, a bright mural depicts the descent in Grandma Moses detail.

In the green mountain valleys of the lower Alps, breathtaking panoramas become a cliché, a treat taken for granted around each corner. These small worlds seem, indeed, to preserve their Alpine heritage in an orderly landscape of pastureland, thick forests, and gentle mountains. But I carried in my mind a magical vision of a wild range of ice-capped peaks, which I had seen shimmering like a mirage on the horizon from the Swiss capital of Bern. I headed for Grindelwald.

Ardent conservationist Kaspar von Almen lives near Grindelwald in perhaps the loveliest green valley of all: Lauterbrunnen. In this valley, ground into a classic U-shape by glaciers, von Almen preserves untouched some 50 acres of woodland. Next to it the family-owned Trümmelbach Falls thunder down through water-sculptured caverns inside a limestone cliff within earshot of his home. "I do not cut anything, I do not introduce anything, I leave it to the trees," said von Almen. "The woods are full of animals which otherwise are hard to see in the valley—badgers, blackcock, chamois in spring and in autumn, and then, of course, red deer. It's amazing how so much animal life can succeed in such a small stretch of woods."

Like most Swiss, he deplores the acid rain drifting over Swiss forests from Europe's industrial chimneys. Pines are particularly vulnerable—and crucial: Pine forests trap and break up the snow, providing the best natural avalanche barriers. National laws protecting forests date back to the end of the 19th century, after timber cutting in the mountains caused disastrous floods and avalanches. Replanting produced the monotonous spruce

Sunlight bathes a golden harvest of cheeses in a mountain clearing above the village of Sigriswil. Here cow owners and sightseers witness an annual ritual: the division of the cheeses. As in other Bernese highland communities, dairymen hired to make mountain cheese keep track of each cow's milk production. At summer's end a proportionate number of cheeses rewards the owner.

A huge crowd celebrates all day with picnics, liberal toasts, and folk music. Virtuoso yodelers match their high-pitched tones against the merry notes of concertinas and the mournful blare of alpenhorns.

Pages 40-41: The Upper Glacier at Grindelwald plunges in frozen motion toward meadows in the valley below. It once reached all the way. In the 19th century visitors could touch the ice and pick strawberries at the same time.

42

forests that modern visitors consider typically Swiss. Several such dark, protective woodlands spread above Grindelwald.

Tourists swarm over Grindelwald. At 3,400 feet it offers easy access to hiking trails and ski slopes beneath the towering peaks of that famous trio of Bernese Alps giants: the Eiger, the Mönch, and the Jungfrau. In the village, building proceeds apace, and tall concrete hotels urbanize the main street. Grindelwald village lacks the rural charm of Château-d'Oex, but the view beyond makes up for it. From green pastures, massive walls of rock reach up to snowy summits. The icy tongues of glaciers creep down gullies in between.

I was carried into that view by one of Switzerland's most spectacular railway rides. From Grindelwald the railroad winds around the flank of the Eiger, the village dwindling below in its green valley. A second rack-and-pinion train, boarded at Kleine Scheidegg, climbs a slope and runs headlong into the side of the Eiger. Between 1896 and 1912, Swiss engineers tunneled $5\frac{3}{4}$ miles upward through solid rock. Passengers doze in the thin air as the track mounts steeply. Twice the train stops for a brief, teasing view from windows cut in the Eiger, then arrives at its destination 11,333 feet up inside the rock saddle between the Jungfrau and the Mönch.

A quick whisk up another 356 feet by elevator, and we emerge in brilliant light and bitter wind on the platform of a silver-domed weather station. Dazzling snowfields undulate into the distance over wave upon wave of mountains. The Aletsch Glacier flows majestically toward a cloud-misted southern range. Above us hangs the icy peak of the Jungfrau. High on the Mönch, three black figures inch their way toward a fourth, who stands at the summit waiting. In this heady world of ice and snow and rock and sky, far above well-tended green farmsteads and valley resorts, nature sheds its 20th-century human burden and the mountains come into their own.

By Mary B. Dickinson
Photographs by Jodi Cobb

It's a bird, it's a plane . . . it's a super skydiving team demonstrating parachuting skills at an international competition in Château-d'Oex. The colorful event is one of many designed to boost Switzerland's all-important tourist economy.

Tourists also attend the fall Schwingfest—wrestling festival—near Aeschi, on a high plateau overlooking Lake Thun. But it's mostly local people, many, like the girl with the straw hat, in traditional dress, who gather to watch friends and relatives compete. Burly contestants don sackcloth shorts and grapple for holds. Each strives to throw his opponent flat on his back in a sawdust ring. The winner's trophy is a decorated cowbell.

At noon the cheerful crowd picnics on fat sausages, ham, beer and wine, and applauds the music of an alpenhorn trio.

A Good Strong Land

Gospel song soars from the picnic shelter into the tall, straight sweet gums, tulips, and sycamores: "Palms of vic-to-ry, crowns of glo-o-ry . . . ."

It rises up the slope toward Mount Le Conte. The song leader lines out each hymn, and then they follow him, altos, basses, sopranos, and baritones harmonizing as if they have been practicing every day. In the back of their minds they have, though they come home to sing together in Greenbrier Cove only this once each spring.

With their song they reclaim the land their grandparents cleared nearly 200 years ago. Their voices lift above the roar of the Middle Prong of the Little Pigeon River, and upstream across the vanished foundation of Vander Bill Whaley's gristmill to the walnut grove that has grown up around the Ownby family cemetery. From the public picnic site on what was Mary Proffitt's farm, where the boys once played ball, the sound floats down past the riverside parking lot that used to be Haynes Whaley's blacksmith shop.

As they rock and sing on Sunday morning and murmur "amen" between hymns, we outsiders can feel the love flowing among the people who come each year to the Greenbrier reunion. It is a love for their God and His music, for each other, and deeply, stubbornly, for the land where they gather.

I cannot imagine that it would have lasted so long if they and their families still held

Time has smoothed the knobs and ridges of the Great Smoky Mountains near Clingmans Dome.

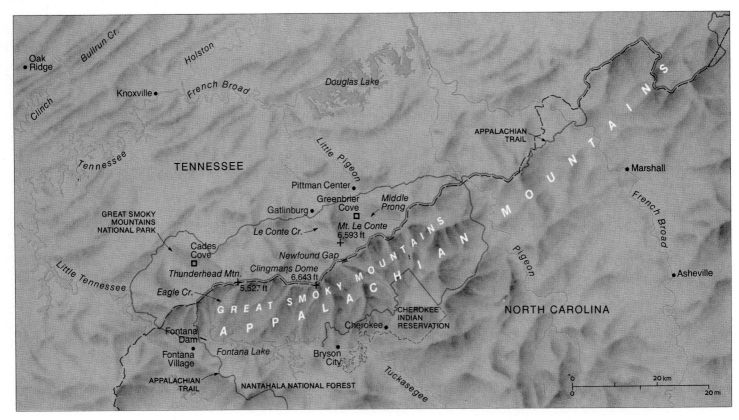

The Great Smokies have drawn generations of people, first Indians and later pioneers. Each wave has left its mark on this unique biosphere, where scientists now measure the continuing impact of humans.

legal title to the land, or had left the cove of their own free will. It is so strong because half a century ago they, their parents, and grandparents had to leave. They were bought out when Congress established the Great Smoky Mountains National Park. And so to them, the familiar mountain tradition of the family reunion also seems a rite of unity against the outside world from which the steep ridges and dense woods shielded them for so long, and a good-natured gesture of defiance against the passage of time.

Nobody says all that, of course. The coming of the park was but one of the pressures brought by the 20th century on the Smokies. Along with the century came high power dams and lakes, highways and encroaching tourist development, and man-made thickening of the haze that gave the mountains their name. Despite all these, the closely managed

Smokies remain unspoiled compared to everything else for hundreds of miles around. Because of the park's unique ecological resources, it is designated a reserve in the Man and the Biosphere Program, an environmental and cultural preservation project begun 17 years ago by the United Nations Educational, Scientific, and Cultural Organization (UNESCO). Specialists monitor what happens to the Smokies' air, water, animals, and plants. This gives a clear baseline from which to measure our further impact on the world.

Some of the families in Greenbrier Cove on homecoming Sunday travel from other states back to their Tennessee roots. Others come barely a few miles up the Little Pigeon.

Carl Whaley begins another hymn. There are no instruments. Carl runs through the verse once, and some of the singers pat their feet in time. There is another, and another, and then as they sing "In the Land Where We'll Never Grow Old," they stand and hug and shake hands with their neighbors.

That is the signal to eat. The women uncover a fantastic variety of casseroles, chicken, biscuits, fresh vegetables, cookies, and pies. As people wander from table to table sampling others' offerings, Carl, who is 75, tells me about the singing tradition. His deep blue eyes and lively eyebrows move as fast as his lips. He explains how he learned "the rudi-ments of music," back when he attended a singing school here in the cove.

Scattered beneath the soaring trees, knots of old-timers catch up with what has happened since the year before. One says his wife doesn't like to come because she always hears about so many who have died.

Haynes Whaley, the blacksmith, is 94. He used to shoe horses in the cove, put on iron wagon tires for 50 cents each. Beside him sits Otis Proffitt, blind and in his 80s. Estel Ownby, who is only 75, says his earliest memory was helping clear pasture and cropland with an ax and crosscut saw. When not clearing, he fished for trout with a cane pole and black crickets, and ran a trapline for possum, coon, and mink.

On and on they talk, loving the sound of each other's voices. There is a steady flow of families in and out of the gathering, coming and going to and from their cemeteries.

They start in early morning, when the old, hand-cut tomb rocks cast long shadows. As the day progresses, other families arrive. They embrace. They clean up the graves beside the lichen-mottled stones, hand engraved with flowers and hearts that remind one of the simple designs of mountain quilts.

Glenn Cardwell is keeper of the lore of the cove. "They used to say if you sat under a cedar, as soon as it got big enough to shade you, you'd die," he says. He and his family moved out when he was a young man, but he bears no grudge against the government. In fact, he is a park ranger; the park has provided a living for him and many others, on and off the government payroll, for many years.

If the government hadn't taken over the park, the lumber companies would have cut it all, he says. "The people who left Greenbrier say you can always buy another farm, but you can't buy good neighbors. That's what they missed." He remembers how the Park Service, in returning the parkland to nature, tried to exert some controls that just never took. Families brought their own plastic flowers to the cemeteries until the park superintendent issued a request that they stop, because the plastic made such a mess. That didn't last much longer than the rule against killing snakes.

Other rules do last, of course. The mountain people are careful about littering or otherwise desecrating the land. So well kept is the park that a scrap of shiny cellophane by the roadside catches the eye a hundred yards away. It likely (Continued on page 53)

Banjo and fiddle combine to make music that is neither bluegrass nor country. "It's old-time buck dance music," says banjo picker Peter Gott, who passes the afternoon with Ernest Franklin. Although the Smokies are within easy reach of the populous East, they still echo with the ballads of Scotch-Irish pioneers who settled here in the late 18th century. With them came a rugged spirit to match the Smokies' rough terrain. Born perhaps 400 million years ago when two continents collided, the Smokies range of the Appalachians are among North America's oldest mountains. They stood for millions of years before the Rockies began to form, and were once perhaps as tall as the Rockies.

Spring brings scattered families back to Greenbrier Cove for their homecoming. Carl Whaley, one of many forced off his land when the Great Smoky Mountains National Park was established in 1934, joins his family over a picnic table. Some 300 former residents and their descendants return—to eat and sing hymns. Others honor ancestors buried in a churchyard at Cades Cove.

Pages 48-49: The Smokies blaze with autumn brilliance. In the half-million-acre park some 130 species of trees grow, more than in all of Europe.

Pages 50-51: Rhododendrons shelter a Smokies creek, one of the more than 330 park streams where rainbow trout and brown trout thrive. These hardy fish, introduced for sports fishing, may squeeze out the native population of brook trout. That competition, combined with loss of habitat, has prompted officials to ban fishing for brookies in the park.

was left by a tourist from afar, unused to the standards here.

Natural litter is another matter. The humus from which the forest springs is deep and fertile in those 180,000 acres of the park where the government arrived in time to save virgin forest. It is thickening again in these coves between the fallen stone walls that used to separate pastures and vegetable plots. Walking up the trail beside the Little Pigeon, I don't appreciate the trees' size until I realize their vertical scale. They are not surprisingly thick for their age. But in climbing for the sun, in only half a century many have shot up a hundred feet and more, and they may reach well past half that height before they send out branches. Their smooth, straight boles lift the bright chirrs and whistles of the spring warblers almost out of earshot for the families leaning over the tombstones below.

In places wild hogs have rutted the mossy floor around the graves, and men's boots tamp the earth back in place. Periwinkle and strawberry runners spread between the stones. "Cemetery vine, that's what they used to call periwinkle," says Glenn Cardwell. He points to a row of small stones. "See how the tomb rocks show when the epidemic was? These rows of children died at the same time. You can almost feel the tears."

Women squat beside stones and trace the faint, crude lettering with their fingers. One points to a stone and tells her daughter, "Now that's your grandma, and this is your mama's aunt over here." One couple back from Virginia looks for the grave of a veteran of the War of 1812. A man finds the marker for a private in the Second Tennessee Cavalry, and strokes it gently as he tells his boy this was his great-grandfather's brother. They recite these ties over and over, as they did last year, and will next year, so their children will not forget them.

The road out of Greenbrier Cove passes within ten miles of Gatlinburg. When the park was created, Gatlinburg had Andy Huff's and Steve Whaley's hotels for hunters,

fishermen, and daring motorists from Knoxville, and Calvin Ogle's and Charlie Ogle's grocery stores. Now Gatlinburg is a solid stretch of motels, souvenir shops, and seasonal traffic congestion. It can be distressing to those who come to the mountains for peace and communion with nature. But even for them, it is an entry point into the wilderness. And it is work for thousands.

Such paradox is true of Gatlinburg, and across the mountains in North Carolina it is true of Cherokee. The town is named for the Indian tribe that was driven west along the infamous Trail of Tears almost 150 years ago. The descendants of those who once hid in the mountains now live on a reservation that cuts into the edge of the park.

They run a procession of moccasin and gem shops and line the roadside with plastic, stuffed, and live bears on exhibit. They take a percentage from high-stakes bingo that draws players from all over the continent. Some of the Cherokees dress in warbonnets and fringed buckskins and charge to pose for photographs. It may seem undignified, but it is a living. Without the highways and the park, there might be none.

This contradiction is true, too, of the dams. We wound for almost three hours over dipping, curving roads to swing around the park, into valleys and past hamlets where lives have been affected and homes inundated by the dams and lakes on the Carolina side.

The greatest of these is Fontana, which backs up the waters of the Little Tennessee to form a broad barrier along the southwest edge of the park. There, in the early forties, thousands of workers converged on a crash project that would generate electricity for something secret (and atomic) at Oak Ridge.

For the workers, the government built Fontana Village, now the site of a secluded lake resort. Aboard a pontoon boat we visit one of the most cheerfully stubborn characters in the whole Little Tennessee Valley. In a cove around the turn into Eagle Creek floats a pale green houseboat bearing the sign Ma-Maw's Place above the door. Ma-Maw Millsaps spreads comfortably on the porch and talks about her family's repeated displacement by the rising waters behind the dam. Past 70, she insists, "Now I'm homesteaded, and I won't have to move no more till I make my final run."

Abruptly another boat cuts around the bend, with a bearded, sunburned man and his towheaded, bright-eyed boy. They are Ma-Maw's son Bob and grandson Robert. Bob, an Army veteran, has been away but came back. "It's hard to get these old hills out of your mind," he says. He is in a club that traps wild hogs, the progeny of escaped European stock that has multiplied to become a threat to park plants and animals. The trappers move hogs across the lake into the Nantahala National Forest, where hunting is allowed. "Those things have got teeth this long," Bob says, holding his fingers wide apart. "Last year we caught more than 300 of them. We hunt bear, deer, and turkey, too."

Bob remembers how the government moved graveyards that would be submerged, and that created "a lot of wild tales about bodies and ghosts." Ma-Maw sometimes hears a noise fluttering in the house, up in the rafters. It always means someone close has died, Bob assures us.

The Millsapses' talk always comes back to the land that once was theirs—and why Ma-Maw is out on a houseboat in Eagle Creek instead of a proper house now far beneath the lake's surface.

"It's probably been a good thing altogether, in the ways of money and jobs and all," she says. "But we were happy before. . . . What they did, they looked your land over and decided what it was worth. They kinda done us like we done the Indians."

Arvel and Jane Greene were moved out by Fontana Lake, too. Now they live in an idyllic hollow on the Carolina side. Along the way there, the forest hangs close over the road. When there is a break in the trees, the view opens up toward Clingmans Dome and Thunderhead. The rising ridges are furred with great hardwoods and undergrown by

Assisted by mule-power, Pete Tipton makes molasses the old way. As a mule turns a press, Tipton feeds in sorghum cane for crushing. The juice is then boiled down to make the fragrant amber syrup once popular as a sweetener throughout the Smokies.

Other mountaineers preserve the time-honored tradition of craftsmanship. Peter Gott scores a log with an ax, in preparation for hewing. Behind him, the first floor of a two-story dwelling begins to take shape. Gott, who settled in the Smokies from Pennsylvania more than two decades ago, shares his craft with others. His students examine the fit of the dovetail notches at the corner of another cabin, as Gott trims a joint with a handsaw.

Pages 56-57: Winter spreads its silent benediction on the homeplace Peter Gott and his family built near Marshall.

Peter and Polly Gott

laurel and rhododendron so thick a bear has a hard time squeezing through.

The Smokies are the highest mountains of the Appalachians and among the oldest on the continent. Erosion has worn them into knobs and ridges gentle by comparison with the younger mountains of the West. Their thickly wooded slopes remind me of Donald Culross Peattie's observation that the mountain man, in these southern Appalachians, is not a real mountaineer, like the highland Swiss—he is a forest man first, even when he is also a farmer.

That describes Arvel Greene. His house is at the end of Bumgarner Branch. The road runs along the Tuckasegee River, then past the Missionary Baptist and Methodist churches opposite the junkyard. Along it are freshly plowed fields, squashed woodchucks, scarecrows newly dressed for the season.

At the end of the road sits what Arvel says "was just an old, throwed-out building" when he moved in during World War II. The house's center section was built just after 1800, of wide, hand-hewn tulip poplar boards. After restoring it, he duplicated that construction in two wings, matching the old boards precisely.

He is that way about wood. "It's been some satisfaction to me when I can just look at the trees. I still like to go where the ax and the saw have never been, and just look at them."

We walk behind his house, past Jane's garden, past the shed with dozens of trapped raccoons' paws nailed on its side. He reminisces. "When I was a boy, we bought no toys; we made them. I made a sliding sled slick as a racer black snake." He made a crossbow and took it hunting squirrels back of Connelly Creek, and accidentally shot his dog, "almost put his eye out."

He used black gum for wheelbarrow wheels because it didn't crack when it dried. "We often used a hollow tree for a beehive. We'd cut a section out, bring it home. . . . We also used it to make feed troughs for stock, cut it in half lengthwise, and cut it that way to make little cradles. But it was chest-

Under the steady hands of the Tuckaleechee Methodist women, scraps of fabric become a quilt. This traditional pattern, Grandmother's Flower Garden, ranks among other favorites, such as Jacob's Ladder and Drunkard's Path. Quilting bees, which give neighbors a chance to visit, are still an important social event in some parts of Appalachia—and they produce bedcovers that will last "from now on," as the mountain people say.

Over the years, isolated Appalachian residents produced most of their own necessities, earning a reputation for self-reliance and exacting workmanship. Keeping that tradition alive, a North Carolina woman coaxes a sleeping cat from a block of wood. To make the business end of a broom, a Tennessee craftsman trims a broomcorn plant. He and five relatives produce and sell some 10,000 handmade brooms a year.

nut that was so plentiful then, before the blight came. . . . It's easy to work into any shape, and durable, almost like locust."

We walk into Arvel's barn. Rather than hay, it is full of wood: The gnarled butt of a walnut tree that grew around a bridge footing. Logs of buckeye. A chunk of quince from Alabama. A stack of hollow Osage orange. Bundles of ash and hickory for tool handles. He knows where each piece is hidden, where it grew, what it might be good for some day. "Some people, it's just born in them I guess, just like to work with wood. . . . It just takes my eyeteeth to throw away a piece I might use for something. My grandson is wood-minded, too, just like me."

As Arvel and I talk, Jane has been in the kitchen. The day is warm, but the kitchen is hot. She is cooking on a wood stove and takes for granted that I will sit for dinner at 11 a.m. All of it has come from her garden, her storehouse where she has infinite varieties of beans and herbs, and from the genuine gravel-scratching, grass-eating chickens and cows out back. She sets the table with chicken pie, mashed potatoes, mustard greens, snap beans, pickled beets, cucumber pickle, corn bread, biscuits, hand-churned butter, rhubarb pie with strawberries baked into it— and this is not Sunday, but Tuesday.

I groan toward a porch swing after eating. It is made of two lengthwise sections of hollow chestnut, matched into an S curve. Beside it Arvel has mounted a carefully sliced round of white oak from a tree that grew 309 years before it was felled. Into its rings he has driven aluminum pins to mark the dates of major events in American history. It will be here after him. He is conscious of posterity. A person cannot live in the hills and fail to be. Only lately have we learned that it may not be this way forever.

The closest watcher of these hills, and therefore the bearer of the bad news, is John Peine. He is director of the Uplands Field Research Laboratory, headquartered in a log cabin by the rustling flow of Le Conte Creek, near Gatlinburg. His crew gathers informa-

Nancy J. Pierce, Black Star

Where their ancestors lived off the land, Cherokee Indians now depend on tourist dollars for a livelihood. One of more than 8,000 Indians on the Cherokee Indian Reservation, Goingback Chiltoskey carves an eagle for sale to visitors. In the town of Cherokee, other Indians offer locally crafted moccasins, pottery, baskets, spears—and even warbonnets, despite the fact that the Cherokees never wore them.

Army troops first routed the peaceable Cherokees from the Smokies in 1838 and forced them west on the Trail of Tears. Some 4,000 people, then about one-fourth of the tribe, died on the march. A few holdouts refused to leave; they hid in the caves and hemlock roughs of the high Smokies until, with time, the federal government said they could stay. The Smokies group became the Eastern Band of the Cherokees; those who settled in Oklahoma became the Cherokee Nation.

Clouds boil from the furrowed Smokies. Now much of the haze is caused by air pollution. Still there is an unspoiled quality to this park: Almost three-fourths of its half million acres are designated as wilderness. Black bears, once hunted almost to extinction, find a haven here, where rhododendrons and a thousand other flowers bloom. The lure of nature attracts millions of city dwellers each year, making the Smokies the nation's most popular park.

David Muench

tion for the Man and the Biosphere Program.

John explains that the natural "smoke" over the Smokies is a haze of moisture and particles emitted by more than 1,500 varieties of trees and plants. What has thickened that haze in recent years is man-made air pollution that does not spare the most remote mountain hollows.

The atmosphere is now thick with sulfates and related materials from coal-fired power plants. Most of the fine particles over these mountains today are man-made. The concentration is from four to twelve times greater than at national parks in the Far West. Because the Smokies are so high, they intercept much of the pollution that drifts eastward from the cities of the Midwest and the Gulf Coast. This mountain range, tallest in the East, suffers the heaviest tree damage. Studies show that moisture combed out of clouds and fog on the high ridges is much more acidic than rain in nearby lower areas.

Among white pines, the species most closely studied here for pollutant damage, 80 percent have been hurt, and 20 percent have suffered severely. The red spruce, "the crown jewel of this crown jewel ecosystem, is under siege, its very survival in doubt," John Peine says. The higher the spruces grow, the more serious the damage, which leads Peine to speculate that the spruces' sickness comes from pollution in the clouds.

In this century man has ravaged the Smokies, then seen what he has done, stopped, pulled back, and protected them. But as the year 2000 approaches, the ultimate insult to the mountains may come from people far away. Because they are not here, they cannot understand how delicate these immovable Smokies are. They have never shoed horses beside the Little Pigeon River, never tracked bear up the hollows above Fontana Dam, looked out from Newfound Gap when the rhododendron is in bloom, or mourned ancestors long gone upon the Trail of Tears.

By Ernest B. Furgurson
Photographs by James P. Blair

Cotton grass brightens the high Canadian Rockies in Jasper National Park.

NATURE ALOFT

Jim Brandenburg

Animals and plants in surprising number and variety make their home on rugged mountainsides. Even on snowcapped peaks, flowers bloom.

In 1889 American scientist C. Hart Merriam, studying Arizona's mountains and deserts, found that certain types of flora and fauna live only within specific temperature-related altitudinal zones. He described a series of life zones ranging from "Tropical" in valleys to "Arctic-Alpine" on high peaks. These zones correspond to the latitudinal zones that occur from Equator to pole. Plants and animals on a high peak resemble those of arctic tundra. We now know that rain, soil, and wind also help determine life zones and often create varied ecological niches within them. Similar zones exist in ranges around the world, from Costa Rica's green slopes to Alaska's icy crags. Africa's Mount Kenya offers an especially clear look at a series of distinct zones.

Ice Caves Astride the Equator

Along a winding path at the base of Mount Kenya—Kere Nyaga, the "mountain of whiteness"—I eventually found him in a cornfield. He lay with his few belongings, cramped in the shadows of a little stick shelter, asleep, or maybe meditating. His name is Ephraim M'Ikiara. Born near the mountain about 60 years ago, he is a carpenter and former farm worker. He is also an incredible mountaineer.

Ephraim M'Ikiara spoke, then looked on strong-eyed while a neighbor interpreted: "He says you must understand that he does not climb for himself. He does not move himself. It is like he sleeps and wakes up to find himself walking."

M'Ikiara walks through a succession of wild forests and moorlands until he is three miles up and naked cliffs surround him. There he rests in caves, waiting to see when he will move again. Above him, the mountain's two enormous spires continue upward, sharp as hyena fangs, making their own storm clouds out of the African sky.

Mount Kenya is a volcano, long quiet, that rises alone at the heart of Kenya. Its base is some 60 miles wide. Like Mount Elgon to the northwest and Kilimanjaro to the south, it formed as Earth's crust spread outward from Africa's Great Rift Valley. Erupting at intervals between 3.1 and 2.6 million years ago, the main vent built a dome perhaps 22,000 feet high. Ice Age glaciers tore it apart. Now

Three miles above the Equator, snow gleams in sunrise on Mount Kenya.

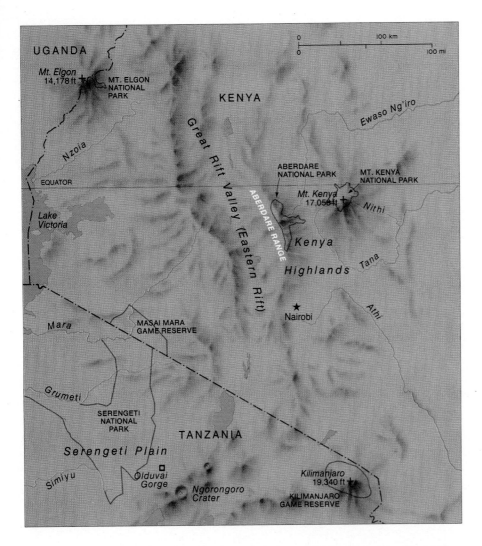

Africa's mountains lie chiefly in separate clusters with different origins, unlike the long, linked ranges of other continents. Geologic ferment that created East Africa's Great Rift Valley millions of years ago also built massive volcanoes along its edges, including Africa's two highest peaks, Kilimanjaro and Mount Kenya. From equatorial base to snowy cap, Mount Kenya displays a distinct series of plant and animal life zones.

the two lava spires—17,058-foot Batian and 17,022-foot Nelion—are the mountaintop, the highest in Kenya, highest on the continent after Kilimanjaro. Once fluid-hot in the volcano's throat, the spires now glitter with ice. Alpinists rate each one much tougher to scale than Switzerland's Matterhorn.

Ephraim M'Ikiara has no climbing companions, no pitons or long coils of rope. He told me that his first several attempts failed but that after he learned the way, he reached Nelion's summit five times. A Mount Kenya National Park warden banked past in a plane and saw him there, a lone form balanced atop the pinnacle—an impossible, barefoot figure clad in shorts and a thin coat.

"It is for God to decide whether he will go again," the interpreter continued, "because it is God who takes him there."

Did he mean the Judeo-Christian God? Or N'Gai, the traditional deity of the Kikuyu people who live around Mount Kenya? Isn't N'Gai said to dwell among the snows of the peak?

"God is God," said Ephraim M'Ikiara, handing me a thumb-worn Holy Bible. "He goes wherever people pray to Him. But He rests here, on Kere Nyaga."

Between this mountain's arctic crown and tropical foot flourishes a remarkable spectrum of plant and animal communities, arranged in horizontal bands—life zones. I wanted to explore each one in detail, beginning at the top and moving downhill, like one of Mount Kenya's many streams. First, however, there was the matter of getting to the top. By the time I reached the uppermost of the huts provided by the Mountain Club of Kenya, I was already starving for oxygen. The next day I finally crested 16,355-foot Point Lenana, just below the twin peaks, clinging to my ice ax in a blizzard less than a dozen miles from the Equator.

The ridge leading off Point Lenana parallels half-mile-long Lewis Glacier, largest of the 11 glaciers still honing the peak. A cave, guarded at its entrance by icicle pillars, led me underneath the ice field. Africa lay suspended in deep blue and absolute stillness.

Ice continues to erode Mount Kenya's double-spired summit, once much higher than the present 17,058 feet of Batian (left spire) and slightly lower Nelion. Lewis Glacier sprawls below them. Climbers first reached Mount Kenya's summit in 1899. Now climbers by the hundreds challenge this craggy peak each year. Plants also struggle to survive in the snow zone. From the sparse soil and shelter of a rock crevice, a tiny groundsel (above) blooms near Lewis Glacier.

Pages 70-71: Author Douglas Chadwick peers into an ice cave hollowed under Lewis Glacier by streaming meltwater and inrushing warm air. Such caves display the rocks and soil—future moraines—that are transported by glaciers.

Pages 72-73: Mist and rain collect in a giant lobelia's rosette of thick leaves, along with a gelatinous antifreeze secreted by the plant. Spiders and insects inhabit this mini-pond, a prime source of food for birds.

Back outside in the shouting wind, the snow zone seemed equally sterile—at first. Hoping to find drinking water, I hacked through five inches of hard ice that coated a tarn three miles above sea level, and swirling threads of green algae welled up out of the hole.

We define what we think organisms need to survive. Then, probing the planet's ultimate reaches, we discover clouds of bacteria in boiling deep-sea vents and insects floating in the stratosphere's jet stream, and we have to expand our definitions again to match the ingenuity of life. It's tough trying to pin down the limits of a miracle.

Orange lichens stippled the rock rubble at the pool's edge. Velvet moss lined seams on the stones' lee side. In deeper cracks where a thin margin of soil collected, wildflowers had taken root. Bright outposts of life, their blossoms danced in the gale even as my fingers turned numb with cold. Tiny rodent tracks, probably made by a brush-furred mouse, wound across the fresh snow from the sheltering underside of one boulder to the next and on *(Continued on page 74)*

past a wooden cross erected in memory of a fallen climber.

I headed downhill the next day into the alpine zone. Although Mount Kenya's nights and mornings are generally clear, clouds pour off the peak each afternoon, as if a caldron of the volcano had been reborn among the black lava spines and talus fields. Before long, I lost my way in heavy fog.

Suddenly I was sure I saw human shapes. I called out to them. None would answer. I called again, and then the wind punched a hole in the mists. "Well, howdy," I mumbled. I'd been hollering at giant groundsels and lobelias. These two types of herbs, closely related to the familiar wildflowers, are towering successes of adaptation to a tropical alpine environment—one in which temperatures vary sharply from day to night but little from season to season.

The groundsel grows as tall as 20 feet. Its very bulk can absorb and store a good deal of the morning sun's heat. Some lobelias grow right from ground level as bulky rosettes, which rise several feet and then produce a column of blue flowers more than three feet tall. In others, the bloom comes wrapped in a blanket of long, hairy, overlapping leaves that resemble ostrich plumes or silvery fur. Now and then, wandering through some lonely tumult of grandeur, I would find myself reaching out to pet one.

When night falls and the glaciers glow with starlight beneath the Southern Cross, the thin air may cool to 20° or even 15°F. But a thermometer placed near the heart of a giant groundsel or lobelia will still read above freezing. Birds probe these warm microhabitats for the insects and spiders attracted to them. Groove-toothed rats burrow upward to make dens within the warmest part of the groundsel stalk.

Not all relationships here are so finely tuned. Elephants crossing between forested valleys sometimes pass through the alpine zone and tear apart acres of groundsels to eat the soft inner tissues. Young lobelia rosettes can be grazed to stubs by the Mount Kenya

rock hyrax, a rabbit-size beast with tusky canines and big, padded, hooflike feet. (Its closest living relative, besides other kinds of hyraxes, just happens to be the elephant.)

Broadest of all the life zones, the alpine belt stretches from about 14,300 feet down to 10,800 feet. Its web of life thickens downslope as the soil does, collecting in the broad valleys scoured out by past glaciers. More and more tussocks of hardy grasses and sedges colonize the frost-heaved ground until they create a kind of tundra, equatorial-style. With different species of groundsels and lobelias, these upper moorlands roll around the mountain, past lava plateaus, craters of old side-vents—the last one blew up around 40,000 years ago—and jade tarns with nesting African black ducks.

Beneath the overlapping tussock heads, where the cold winds can't reach and dead stalks mulch the earth for tiny wildflowers, bustles a neighborhood of mice, shrews, crested rats, mole rats, little alpine meadow lizards, and a type of viper known only from Mount Kenya. Coveys of pheasant-like francolins strut by, pecking at weevils and grass buds. Meanwhile, common duikers—small antelope scarcely taller than the tussocks they graze—add protein to their diet by eating francolin eggs and chicks.

Crossing to the comparatively dry northern slope, I hiked among much larger grazers: mixed bands of eland and Burchell's zebra. When I parted the tussocks, I met lion prints. The high, open slopes and their food chains—each scent, each scurry—became more alive than ever in my mind.

Below 11,000 feet the soil develops a peaty organic layer. It is too acid and boggy to be very fertile. But combined with warmer average daily temperatures—the rule of thumb is a 3° to 5°F increase for every 1,000-foot decrease in altitude—it begins to support thickets of woody plants across the moorlands.

This is the heath zone, dominated by shrubs of the heather family, plants with tough, flexible stems whose branches are hung with narrow evergreen leaves and

Alpine survival tactics sustain both plants and animals. Soft fronds blanket tiny flowers on the giant lobelia's five-foot-tall stalk (left and far left). The giant groundsel's leaf cluster (upper) opens with the rising sun—and a scarlet-tufted malachite sunbird arrives to breakfast on the insects living inside. A Mount Kenya rock hyrax (above), a large and long-furred subspecies unique to this mountain, basks in the sun's welcome warmth.

white flower bells. Awash in afternoon mists, the higher reaches of Mount Kenya's shrub fields might easily be mistaken for a stretch of Scotland's moors. Such similarities often exist between the life zones of high altitudes and high latitudes. By contrast, the lower reaches of Kere Nyaga's heath zone provide another example of tropical giantism as the heaths grow to the height of modest trees.

Down toward 10,000 feet—the farthest reach of the Ice Age glaciers—frost is less frequent, soils are better drained. And the giant heaths suddenly give way to a forest of large East African rosewood trees mixed with giant forms of the herb Saint-John's-wort. Like most groundsels and lobelias, most Saint-John's-worts are ordinary little wildflowers. Here, two species stand up to 40 feet tall.

Biologists speak of "edge effect" to describe the extra diversity of life where two adjoining ecosystems meet and mingle. The open rosewood forest, a narrow belt between the moorlands and the dense woodlands below, is an especially rich sort of edge.

I climbed a stout rosewood branch that leaned out over a grassy glade. The air was lush and shadow-woven, murmuring with bees in the rosewood's pink flower sprays and blossoming with swallowtail butterflies. Scarlet-tufted malachite sunbirds sipped nectar from the orange blossoms of Saint-John's-worts while bushbuck and waterbuck slipped quietly by. The place felt so sheltering and softly green. I had only my sun-blistered nose and wind-cracked lips to remind me of the harsh sweep of highlands I'd just left behind.

The forest floor glowed with scarlet gladioli and red-hot poker lilies. Portions sprouted elderberry and nettles, which tend to invade habitats disturbed by grazing and trampling. A powerful scent confronted me, and I stopped dead quiet. Somewhere close, testing my own scent, stood Cape buffalo; stood massive black horns and shoulders; stood aggressive temperaments that come full charge when things go badly. The ground trembled, from heavy hooves moving . . . away.

Like a forest in a futuristic film, giant groundsels loom over a porter along the Naro Moru Track to Point Lenana, just below the rugged twin peaks. Campsites, lodges, and guided hikes await visitors at 227-square-mile Mount Kenya National Park. Tempted by this relatively easy trail, some visitors hike and scramble to Point Lenana in one day—and fall victim to altitude sickness.

Pages 78-79: The Nithi River cuts a thousand-foot-deep path through Gorges Valley, one of seven main river valleys that cleave Mount Kenya's slopes. These ravines provide mild, sheltered habitats for a wide variety of plants and animals.

Twisting branches inscribe a misty sky (above) and scarlet gladioli brighten the day in Mount Kenya's lush rosewood zone, a narrow belt of open forest extending from about 9,500 to 10,000 feet. Higher lies the dramatically different heath zone and rocky moors and ridges, adorned with such flowering herbs and shrubs as thistle (right, upper) and pink orchids (center). Below the rosewood forest, another distinct life zone begins: Dense bamboo (opposite), growing as tall as 50 feet, creates a shadowy world of its own.

In every habitat the traveler may suddenly encounter a sparkling cascade as Mount Kenya sends life-giving water to the plains below.

At the bottom of the rosewood-Saint-John's-wort belt, I followed a bull elephant as he rumbled across a grassy clearing and began stripping leaves from a taller type of grass—bamboo—at the meadow's edge. Then he vanished completely into the bamboo. So did I, guided by a local farmer, Godfrey Mugambe, who cuts wood and keeps beehives in Mount Kenya's forests.

On the dry northern slopes the mountain bamboo appears as scrubby clumps among East African pencil cedar and a yew-like conifer. But on the wet eastern and southeastern slopes, where prevailing winds from the Indian Ocean drop as much as 100 inches of rain annually, the bamboo grows in almost pure stands in a zone between about 9,400 and 7,900 feet. Following the elephant trails that wound there among stalks 40 and 50 feet tall, I felt like a bug at the bottom of some titanic grass tussock.

Underfoot, mole rats burrowed through the deep leaf litter. Overhead, troops of Sykes' monkeys shook the canopy, feeding on new bamboo leaves; finchlike Abyssinian crimson-wings whistled tunes. But I rarely saw any of them. In the dank, all-encompassing green gloom, I couldn't even find the sky to tell the time of day or weather in the world outside—only more crisscrossed stalks to squeeze past. Okay, maybe a wide-frame backpack hadn't been such a brilliant choice for this expedition. From the sounds around Godfrey and me, the animals weren't having an easy time either. When elephants or buffalo—what was *that*? black rhino?—crashed too close by, we would start whacking our machetes against a hollow dead stem to let them know we were there.

Pointing with his blade, Godfrey showed me a huge, pinkish fungus ball weighing down a dead or dying stalk. "Good for making soup," he said. Pink toadstools rose from the elephant dung. When night fell, the entire forest floor glimmered with elfin lights from phosphorescent molds.

The next afternoon, clammy to the bone in a drizzling rain, we reached the eastern

An elephant eyes a photographer high on Mount Kenya. Found chiefly on lower slopes, elephants also wander into the alpine zone, where they pull down giant groundsels to feed on the juicy innards.

Isak Dinesen in 1937 told of elephants in Kenya "travelling through dense native forest . . . pacing along as if they had an appointment at the end of the world." A few decades later, hunting and habitat destruction had brought numbers drastically low; the appointment was clearly with extinction. Kenya banned elephant hunting in 1972 (and in 1977 ended all big-game hunting). But poachers still take a heavy toll and woodcutters continue to clear the forests.

slope's conifer-forest zone, which begins below the bamboo. Mist-wet strands of lichen, another fungus, draped the branches. Black-and-white colobus monkeys plucked it off by the handful to eat. The long fur of their white shoulder-capes and tails matched the pale lichen perfectly.

Close by on another branch hunched the dark shape of a crowned eagle, a hunter of monkeys. Turacos with amethyst plumage set up a raucous screeching that was passed along from tree to tree. Toward evening, deeper bird cries carried over this montane rain forest as green ibis flew home in lavender twilight to roost.

I hoped to glimpse the shy, largely nocturnal striped antelope, the bongo. Instead, I saw zebra in striped woodland sunlight. I tried to locate the Cape clawless otter. Instead, I found a streamside family of giant forest hogs and a serval cat. I wanted to circle on in this way day after day, on the wild edge of surprise. And I did. Great Kere Nyaga, a mountain of niches, was beginning to seem like the whole world to me.

Conifers can persist on drier slopes nearly down to the thirsty plains, since their slender waxy needles offer little surface for water loss through evaporation. On the lower wet slopes, at around 6,500 feet, a rain forest of towering broad-leaved trees replaces them.

Here is the most complex life zone of all, with a monumental overstory of species such as pillarwood and East African camphorwood, middle-story trees such as East African olive, and an array of understory shrubs, including wild coffees and herbs. Mosses carpet the trunks. Ferns feather outward from the moss colonies. Vines twist between trees and down from the fern-laden branches to head-high fern copses on the dim forest floor. The air is hot, humid, and close, smelling equally of growth and of sweet-sour decay, filled with whisperings—the breath of true tropical jungle.

This part of Africa was brand new to me. As before, elephant trails proved to be the best routes through the forest tangle. But now the dung writhed with insect larvae and parasitic worms. Mosquitoes drilled through the dusk. Suddenly it was night, jungle night, and I began to understand the worship of fire. I stoked the flames, remembered the fresh leopard spoor we had seen, and stoked the flames higher.

Yet while big critters rip through the imagination, the worst enemy of sleep turns out to be the little tree hyrax. Its nighttime call, a proclamation of territorial rights, is a whopping grunt—*BWAHP*—followed by a scream like that of a far larger being—a hysterical dinosaur, perhaps. It can be heard a mile away. All night. Then as red-eyed dawn arrives, black-and-white colobus monkeys start roaring from the boundaries of each troop's range.

The farther downhill I went, though, the more often muddy logging roads crossed the elephant paths and the sound of chain saws sliced through animal cries. I met a cutting crew by one road and, since I do some logging around my Montana cabin, we compared notes. It turned out that we used the same brand of chain saw. But I never had to sharpen mine after felling just one tree, as they told me they must with the ultradense Meru oak. Nor had I ever worked in a pit on a two-man team turning hardwood logs into boards with a long handsaw.

Mount Kenya National Park, established in 1949, protects mainly the crags and high moorlands. Its lower boundary circles the mountain at 10,500 feet, with only two narrow extensions to lower areas. Below this boundary, the forest zones down to 6,890 feet lie within the Mount Kenya Forest Reserve, which is managed, like national forests in the United States, under a multiple-use policy. Timber is the chief economic resource.

With the Forest Department regulating the amount of timber cut, Mount Kenya's woodlands aren't disappearing. But they are changing fast. Heavy logging has made old-growth habitats rare. Pencil cedar of any age, prized as fencing material for its rot-resistant qualities, is harder to find. After certain lower slopes are clear-cut and burned, the government permits farmers to plant crops on them for three years. Foresters then replant the land with trees, but they tend to favor fast-growing, non-native pine, cypress, and eucalyptus. Livestock grazing, which is permitted in the reserve, can also alter the balance of native forests.

As such disturbances increase, they affect both the wildlife tied to specific forest zones and wider-ranging animals that also use the park. Kenya conservationists are equally concerned that human activities might damage the mountain's vital role as a water catchment. Kere Nyaga not only makes its own precipitation but also stores it like a giant sponge. An intact native forest can absorb a tremendous amount of rainfall in its humus layer, releasing a steady flow to the streams. Where cutting, grazing, and farming occur, rainfall runs off more quickly, eroding soils and their nutrients and leaving a less dependable water supply for the dry seasons.

What else may be lost? Wangombe Muchiki, a 65-year-old Kikuyu, took me for a stroll through his personal pharmacy—the woods. "Boil the roots of this vine, and the tea will cure stomach worms. These leaves," he continued, holding up a yellow-flowered herb I had stepped over, "make the blood strong. Charcoal from rosewood brings down swelling. This one heals cuts. . . ." When it comes to the uses of tropical plants, science is only beginning to catch up to folk wisdom.

Not long ago, Mount Kenya's wild forests served still another purpose. During the violent Mau Mau uprising against colonial rule in the 1950s, they became a major stronghold for the guerrillas. Kenya gained independence from Great Britain in 1963. Today peaceful fields cover almost every square foot of the slopes below the Forest Reserve.

One afternoon I visited Godfrey Mugambe at his *shamba*, the farmstead that he and his wife and children work, together with his two brothers and their families. The daily chores of weeding and watering were suspended while we sat holding hands with the children

and talking. We shared a meal of potatoes, beans, maize, and tea, all just picked from the fertile volcanic soil with its abundant minerals. I could make out coffee fields above the shamba, mango and banana trees below. As storm clouds flowed out from the peak, sunlight reached in beneath them, silvering two streams—the shamba's water sources—that converged at the foot of the hill. Truly, as the mountaineer Ephraim M'Ikiara had told me, those who live close to Kere Nyaga are especially blessed.

Along with its many resources, Kenya also has one of the world's highest birthrates, with an average of eight children per family. The nation's resources will have to be divided among twice as many people within just 20 years from now. Clearly, the challenge here, as in so much of the world, is to find room somehow for both human and wildland communities.

Except on the rainy, hilly eastern side, the landscape quickly turns browner as Mount Kenya at last levels onto the plains between 5,000 and 4,000 feet. There are fewer fields and fewer people, and more of them are carrying water on their backs. The change is most dramatic to the north, where all the bushes on the tapering slopes suddenly seem to have thorns and burrs.

Then the true savanna takes over. It is the Africa of thin-spiked acacias with weaverbird nests hung from them, swinging in the hot wind; of parched grasses dependent solely on seasonal rains—rains that sometimes fail. Thin cattle and goats graze and tread the brittle grasses to powder until, as on the heights, naked rock lies exposed to the sun.

I could see those heights. Looking back through the heat waves and dust, I saw mile upon mile and layer upon layer of green rising in the air. Above, clouds were building on the glacier-colored summit of the mountain from which the nation of Kenya takes its name.

By Douglas H. Chadwick
Photographs by George F. Mobley

Where forests once grew, tea terraces now scallop Mount Kenya's lowest slopes, outside the national park boundary. Here volcanic soil and generous rainfall create some of Kenya's richest farming land. The cool highland climate produces a slower growing and thus more flavorful tea, a major export crop. The tea plant's spreading roots, along with the system of terracing, help control erosion.

Tender tea shoots must be picked by hand (above). But laborers abound in Kenya, which has one of the world's highest birthrates. Rapid population growth keeps the nation's leaders under pressure to clear more and more highland forests for agriculture.

Caribou bulls tangle antlers in Alaska's Denali National Park.

Wild Domains

Every year in May the caribou cross Alaska's Denali National Park and Preserve en route to summer pastures south of the Alaska Range. Through mountain passes, over trails worn by centuries of migration, the females move in a herd of hundreds; the bulls and yearlings follow later. But the caribou migration, covering hundreds of miles, is only the most conspicuous display of the park's large animals. Dall's sheep, moose, wolves, and grizzlies also feature in this six-million-acre wilderness. In all, nearly 200 mammal and bird species coexist in a fragile, subarctic environment.

Mount McKinley, the highest peak in North America, towers over the landscape. A prospector named it after soon-to-be President William McKinley in 1896, but the Indians knew it as Denali, "the high one." And high it is, soaring to 20,320 feet, 18,000 of them above its base. Few mountains in the world so thoroughly command the surrounding terrain. (In height from base to peak, McKinley dwarfs Mount Everest, which rises only 12,000 feet.)

The land McKinley dominates is giant-size too: huge glacial valleys, wide outwash plains, awesome gorges, twisting glacier-fed rivers, and everywhere the peaks on peaks of the Alaska Range, a crescent-shaped chain reaching 600 miles across Alaska.

Beginning some 65 million years ago, the Denali Fault sys-

90

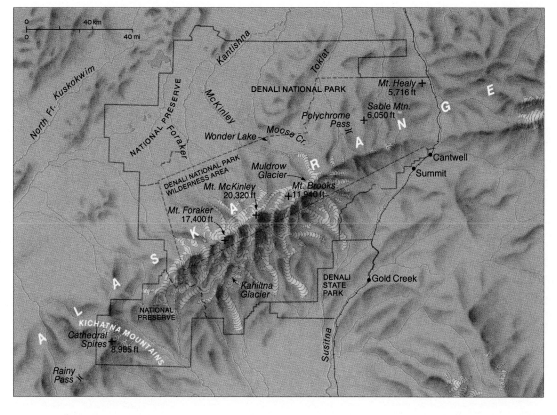

Denali National Park and Preserve straddles the Alaska Range 250 miles south of the Arctic Circle. Larger than Massachusetts, Denali includes the former Mount McKinley National Park—now a wilderness area—and other lands added by Congress in its 1980 Alaska Lands Act. Mount McKinley, the park's glacier-packed centerpiece, presides over a domain of nearly 200 bird and animal species that eke out a precarious existence.

tem rumpled a flat lowland and created this massive hodge-podge of peaks. Stretching from the Alaska Peninsula to the Canadian border, the fault—North America's largest—passes through the area, occasionally jolting the park with tremors.

Glaciers have eroded and sculptured the mountains and still cling to many of their flanks. Mount McKinley alone has 17 major glaciers, 4 of them more than 25 miles long. McKinley takes the moist air blowing north from the Gulf of Alaska and wrings snow from it, feeding the glaciers. Thus, clouds often obscure the mountain's twin summits. Only a fraction of the 400,000 or so visitors from around the world who

come each year hoping for a look at McKinley actually get one. The mountain dominates conversations: "Is it out?" people ask, and everyone knows what they are talking about.

Much of the park lies north of McKinley and its neighboring peaks, on the leeward side of the range. In this rain shadow, precipitation averages a scant 15 inches a year. But melting ice and snow from the mountains feed lowland streams.

At lower elevations in the park, especially along bottomlands, stunted spruces grow from a dense, spongy carpet of mosses and lichens. In drier areas, white spruce mixes with quaking aspen, paper birch, and balsam poplar. This often

sparse growth is called taiga, a Russian word meaning "land of little sticks." Here, in the thin topsoil, shallow-growing roots cannot support the tall tree trunks of more temperate forests. At times the waterlogged topsoil slips downslope, giving the taiga an often mentioned look of a drunken forest.

At higher elevations—around 2,700 feet in the park—the taiga gradually gives way to tundra, a treeless landscape. Exposed slopes above the tree limit catch the full brunt of winds that drive ice and snow in the winter and sandblast the scenery in summer. The contorted branches of dwarf shrubs attest to the torment. But scores of tiny wildflowers—some of

Betty Sederquist

the area's nearly 450 plant species—have adapted to the freezing temperatures and short growing seasons. In summer, the moss campion, mountain avens, alpine azalea, and forget-me-not put on a dazzling display as they spread out like rugs in the sunlight.

In the realm of tundra and rock, sure-footed Dall's sheep rule the ridges, their white coats plain against the brown and black slopes. Moose browse in the ponds and willow thickets of the taiga forest. Denali's largest residents, the bulls can weigh up to 1,800 pounds and reach a shoulder height of seven feet. Like Dall's sheep and caribou, they joust every autumn for the right to breed with

females. Then, loud cracking sounds reverberate through the park as antlers clash.

Wolf packs roaming this sub-arctic wilderness prey on moose, caribou, sheep, and small mammals—usually the old or young or injured. Grizzlies amble along, eating almost anything they see. They may dig for hours to unearth an arctic ground squirrel's burrow—while the squirrel watches from another exit. Red foxes dart about in search of mice, lemmings, snowshoe hares, and willow ptarmigan.

Overhead, golden eagles soar and swoop for small mammals and birds. More than 150 bird species live in the park. Most fly south in the fall, the golden-

plover to the Southern Hemisphere and the arctic tern all the way to Antarctica.

In 1917 Congress set up the park to protect wildlife from hunters traveling on the nearly completed Alaska Railroad. Then Congress in 1980 almost tripled the park's size and, in deference to the Indians, changed its name (though not the mountain's) from Mount McKinley to Denali. But the mountain's increasing popularity brings new concerns: trash and safety. More than 700 people a year set out to conquer McKinley, though the subarctic conditions send half of them back before reaching its peak.

By Elizabeth L. Newhouse

Twin forks of a glacier grind through the Alaska Range, shaping a striped river of ice streaked with debris from the slopes. Dozens of glaciers spawn in these mountains, nourished year after year by fresh snow that eventually compresses to ice. When glaciers converge, as they do here, the accumulated debris forms a wide central swath known as a medial moraine. In time, it will be a long, thin embankment.

Dall's sheep graze atop a ridge at the foot of Sable Mountain.

Tom Bean

The Cathedral Spires: hallelujahs in granite amid the Alaska Range.

Betty Sederquist

96

Rick McIntyre

Galen Rowell

At 20,320 feet, Mount McKinley stands as North America's highest peak. Such a view is rare, especially in the summer when clouds often cling to the slopes. George Vancouver, the 18th-century English navigator who first described the Alaska Range, wrote of "distant stupendous mountains covered with snow." Today hundreds of climbers scale McKinley each year, often braving sub-zero temperatures and winds that can reach 100 miles an hour.

But Denali also belongs to its wildlife—to the raven that leaves wing prints as it struggles to take flight from the soft, deep snow; and to the grizzly plucking soapberries before another winter's hibernation.

MONTEVERDE

In the Clouds of Costa Rica

Well, here goes. I draw up my knees and my feet lift off the forest floor. On a slender rope I dangle from a branch seventy feet overhead. I pull myself upward. Two feet. Five feet. Ten, twenty, forty. Don't look down. At seventy feet a camp cot hangs from a limb like a swing; I work my way up to its edge, turn gingerly, and sit.

"You made it!" Nalini greets me as she dangles her feet over the side. Nalini Nadkarni and I have climbed to the canopy of a forest on a mountain in Costa Rica, she to study its plants and animals, I to wonder at a lofty otherworld barely glimpsed from the ground. Hour upon hour this research biologist from California sits up here on her cot, watching the plants and creatures of the canopy work out the intricate equation of life.

And what an equation it is. Lichens and mosses upholster every trunk and branch; orchids and bromeliads turn every cranny into a window box. Emerald toucanets pluck fruits with their scimitar beaks as hummingbirds in electric hues loot the honeypots of countless blooms. Through a break in the foliage we gaze 60 miles westward to clouds strewn like pillows on the polished Pacific.

Suddenly everything goes white. We sit in mist and silence. Then the mist lifts, the colors return. We are just downslope from the mountaintop, and the summit's resident

Cloud mist bathes a mountaintop jungle in the Monteverde Cloud Forest Reserve.

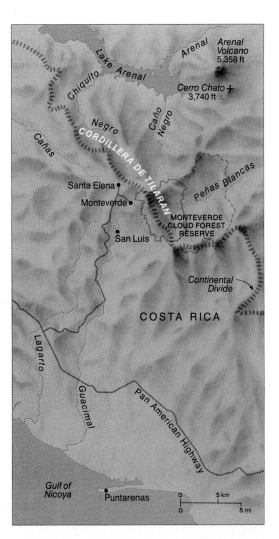

A bridge between continents, a wall between seas, Central America thrusts up volcanic peaks that make Costa Rica a wrinkle of ridges and valleys. Here the winds and storms of two oceans meet, the Pacific to the west and the Atlantic beyond the Caribbean Sea to the east. Here ecosystems interact as the isthmus links temperate North America to warmer, wetter South America. And here volcanoes like Arenal spit and growl, each a red bead on the Pacific's necklace of lava caldrons—the Ring of Fire.

Born of such forces, a rich array of plant and animal life awes visitors to Monteverde Cloud Forest Reserve and a larger tract now being set aside to the east (dashed line).

cloud bank is doing push-ups on its jungle rug. This is the edge not of rain forest but of cloud forest, a dripping jungle misted by the moisture wrung from ocean winds as they whoosh up the flanks of the Tilaran Cordillera in northwestern Costa Rica. A jungle aptly named Monteverde. Green Mountain.

Rain keeps it green from May to November as wet winds pile out of the Pacific all morning and build thunderstorms by midafternoon. In November the Atlantic trade winds take over, and by the time they climb the ridge from the east, the clouds they bring

have little rain left. Yet even in the dry spell between Christmas and Easter it "rains" in the forest as the cloud mist condenses on millions of leaves and drips to the ground.

Nearby I spot an old friend. A begonia—not the pampered invalid withering on my Virginia windowsill but an exuberant geyser of pink bubbling out of a treetop knothole. Familiar shapes surround me: the green hearts of a philodendron, the spiky asterisk of a bromeliad. Houseplants back home, they flourish here in wild abandon a mile above sea level and 70 feet off the ground.

Nalini climbs her ropes to learn how they do it. They grow as epiphytes, she explains, so-called air plants that thrive aloft with no roots to the ground. Nowhere are these amazing plants more abundant or diverse than in the cloud forests of Latin America. A single tree may support 100 species, a velvet coat so full you can barely glimpse an inch of the tree itself. Yet epiphytes are not parasites; they take no food from the host tree. They let the great trees do the growing toward sun and rain while they perch on the trunks and branches and share the benefits of life aloft.

Up here in the canopy the sunlight blazes; only scattered sparks of it slip through to the ground. Here dust and rain bestow precious nutrients; the groundlings get the leftovers. But it's no free ride for the epiphytes. Nalini has found that the host trees send out roots from their branches to collect a rent of nutrients from the thick mats of plants and debris.

Thunder rumbles beyond the ridge. "Hear that?" Nalini says. "Arenal." So it wasn't thunder but a growl from Arenal Volcano, one of Costa Rica's many lava caldrons. Flow by flow, ash fall by ash fall, the hot-hearted planet has built up this mountain ridge and robed it in good volcanic soil.

Yet most of the nutrients are not in the soil but in the living vegetation. When a tree falls and rots, it quickly recycles into new leaves and stems and blooms. Thus most of the trees here do not send down deep taproots; instead they spread a web of roots close to the surface where most of the nutrients lie.

Treetops near the Continental Divide look down on approaching clouds. As humid ocean winds climb the ridge, moisture condenses into clouds that soak the summit in rain and mist. In one 18-month span, gauges recorded 95 percent humidity every day but one.

William E. Thompson, Earth Images

Pages 102-103: Arenal Volcano spouts a plume of smoke from a throat bubbling with lava. Cerro Chato dozes nearby, trees lining a crater that once boiled like Arenal's. On the far ridge the forests of Monteverde, rooted in the dust of old eruptions, enjoy a rare cloudless day.

Nicholas DeVore III

Pages 104-105: Golden toads roil a pool in a breeding frenzy. Several males clasp the dark females in a grip called amplexus; there they ward off rivals until time to mate. Unknown to science until 1964, these two-inch-long amphibians live nowhere else on earth—a find that helped win protection for their mountaintop habitat.

Michael and Patricia Fogden

Costa Rica is a small country, but it stands tall among nations that guard their natural treasures. A tenth of its land is in national parks and reserves, a ratio few other nations can match. But unprotected habitats continue to vanish as trees are felled for lumber or new pastureland. Because habitats interlock, a protected area can still be damaged by what happens miles away. And the cutting goes on, even as government and private programs preach the wisdom of conservation.

Around me sprawls a living dividend of that wisdom: the Monteverde Cloud Forest Reserve, 17,000 acres saved by Costa Rican law, by Alabama Quakers—and by toads.

Singing fills a Quaker schoolhouse not far from Nalini's tree. Out the windows floats a hymn, unsteady in harmony but anchored in the bedrock of Quaker belief, which holds that war is abhorrent in the sight of God. Such faith led a community of immigrants to this mountainside three decades ago.

"Dona nobis pacem," they sing. Give us peace. But their native America did not give them peace. In 1948 it ordered its young men to register for the (Continued on page 106)

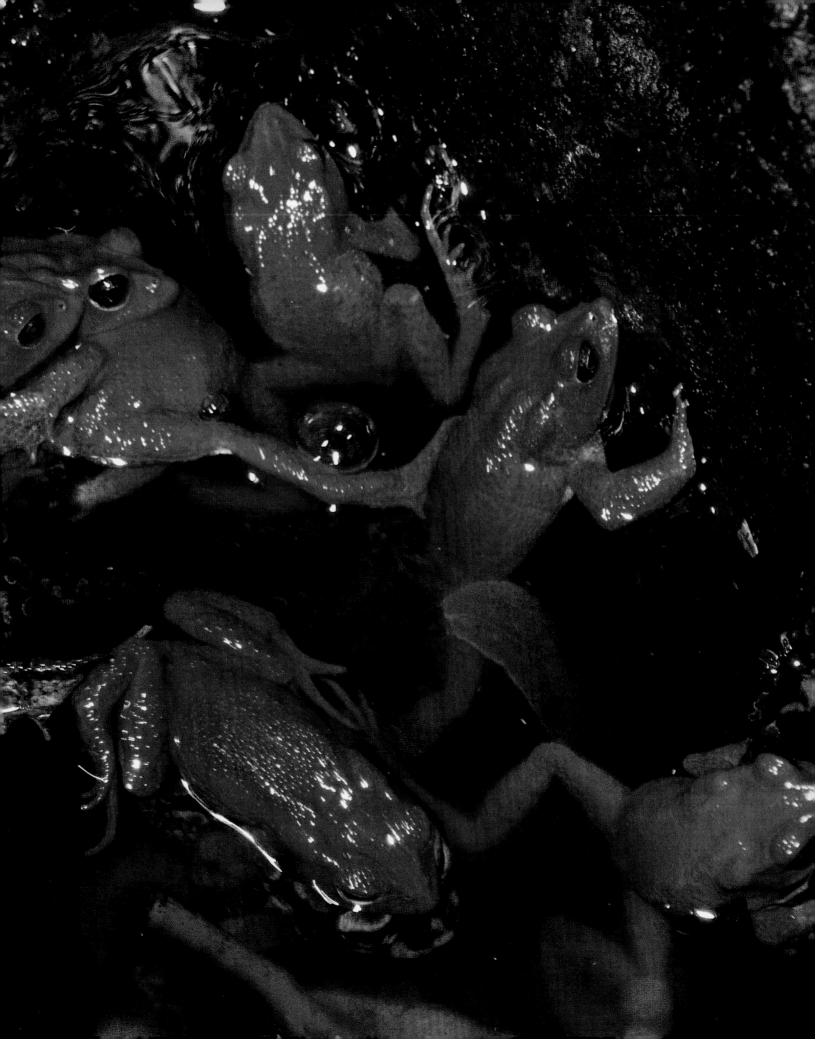

military draft. And in Fairhope, Alabama, four young men said no.

Dreary months in jail gave them time to think about corners of the world where Quakers might farm and worship and never hear the sabers rattle. Costa Rica had just abolished its army; could this nation half the size of Kentucky be the haven they sought?

A delegation flew down to see. On this isolated crest they saw a mosaic of pasture and forest that might do for dairying. Seven families pulled up stakes and struggled southward to hack out a settlement on the ridgepole of Central America. They bought 3,000 acres and named their new home Monteverde. It's still their home today.

Some of them were barely out of their teens. Now these are in their fifties and sixties, and you can read in their faces the hardships they endured. The only way to get their jeep up the mountain was to wrap a chain around a tree and winch it up, one tree after another, along an old ox path. When they got stuck, the Costa Rican farmers brought out ox teams and pulled them free. And when food ran short, they hunted monkeys, owls, even the lethargic sloths that ooze along the branches in perpetual slow motion.

The immigrants cleared land and kept it fertile by letting the big trees rot where they fell, while cattle munched grass in between. From the Ticos—so the Costa Ricans call themselves—the Quakers bought milk to add to their own in a cheese-making operation that has been the mainstay of the mountain folk, both Tico and gringo, ever since.

As they laid out their farms, the pioneers set aside a thousand acres of forest on the ridge to protect their watershed. They'd never heard of an epiphyte. But scientists who study such things began to realize later that the Quakers had padlocked a living treasure chest—and in it a creature new to science, a species of toad found in a single square mile of this ridge and nowhere else in the world: the brilliant little golden toad.

Most toads hop through life in humdrum shades of unisex brown. Not the golden; the

Life dances to simple rhythms for a community perched in the clouds. The reward of morning milking brightens the smile and stretches the arm of Tami Rockwell (opposite), whose Quaker parents left Alabama to help found the Monteverde settlement in 1951. Milk rides horseback but farm children walk (lower left), bundled against morning winds as they deliver milk to the cheese factory. Begun by Quakers, the factory now buys most of its milk from Costa Rican farmers. Another founder, bearded Wilford Guindon, circles with fellow Quakers, scientists, Costa Rican neighbors, and tourists at the settlement's school and meetinghouse, where a square dance every other Saturday bonds friendships and lightens the labors of dairying. Between dances and Sunday meetings, the school educates children from the community and nearby Costa Rican villages—including a lad whose fingers seek music in the strings of a homemade guitar.

males wear bright yellow-orange, the females black and scarlet. Even so, hungry snakes have a hard time finding them as they hide under leaves and roots. And so do visitors, for these rare amphibians seldom come out of hiding except in their short breeding period. But when the dry season ends and the rains make puddles, out come the goldens, as many as 50 to a pool, all scrambling for a chance to mate.

Some call this one of nature's most striking mating displays. But in a week or two it ends, and again the golden toads hide their brilliance under the litter on the forest floor. To glimpse just one, of either sex, is a memorable experience, for many say the goldens are the most beautiful toads in the world.

The toad and its habitat had to be saved. People in Costa Rica and the United States poured money into the effort. Today the Monteverde Cloud Forest Reserve embraces the land the Quakers set aside and 16,000 acres more, all managed by the privately run Tropical Science Center in San José, the capital.

In this warm, wet climate, plants flourish in incredible diversity. Some 500 species of trees have been counted in the reserve. And since animal life responds to plant resources, an amazing array of creatures has evolved. Bats alone number 32 species, including 10 that eat fruit and 7 that sip nectar by night as 30 kinds of hummingbirds do by day. One scientist has tallied more than 500 species of butterflies—and he's still counting.

Trails in and around the reserve lace together not one forest but a museum of forest types, each the creation of wind and cloud and a particular fold of terrain. The Sendero Pantanoso, the "swamp trail," leads hikers in rubber boots through a sodden jungle where orchids nod as the intruders brush past and unseen tree frogs ping like one-note xylophones. The ridge's flat plateau cannot drain well, so it lies like a sponge under a sprinkler. In its dark tangle much of life is lived soaking wet. To some botanists it's no wonder the philodendron's leaf tapers to a sharp "drip tip," an adaptation, they think, that drips

Small but deadly, a black-spotted palm viper (left) curls among ferns of the cloud forest. Though its life in the trees keeps it from underfoot, wise hikers watch for it as they pass low branches and shrubs. In open woods downslope, birdwatchers revel in a favorite sighting: the male resplendent quetzal (above). Now protected, this endangered species may yet vanish as ranchers and land speculators clear the trees from its high-country habitat.

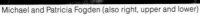
Michael and Patricia Fogden (also right, upper and lower)

water off before fungi can sprout on the leaf.

The bromeliads do the opposite; the funnel at the base of the leaves collects a pool that supplies water to the shallow-rooted plant—and a home to myriad guests. Bacteria and insect larvae swarm in the tiny goblet; tadpoles writhe about, hatched there from eggs laid by tree frogs. An entire micro-community can thrive in the heart of a bromeliad.

Insects and reptiles abound in the soaking swamp. Look down: A snake scoots up the trail with a hapless salamander in its mouth. A grim column of army ants ripples along in search of katydids, cockroaches, anything that moves. Listen: A three-striped warbler twitters in a berry bush. Something grunts up ahead, a loud croak like a human belch. A tapir? Possibly—but hunting the piglike tapir and clearing its forest habitat outside the reserve have made it rare inside as well.

Oddly, birds and mammals seem scarce, as if the dense foliage hides the hundreds that must be there. But many *are* scarce here, and science still ponders exactly why. Yet they are never far away. A migration of a mile downslope or along the ridge takes them out of the swamp and into another forest type.

The Sendero Brillante, the "brilliant trail," lets hikers switch habitats too as it takes them to the elfin forest. Here the land plunges eastward from the ridge, and trees in miniature crouch and cling to it, gnarled and stunted by winds that can knock a hiker flat. Here and there a lone oak tree pokes its head above the others, its foot splayed into buttresses against the shearing force. No need to dangle on a rope; in some places you can stand on the gloomy, tangled forest floor and almost touch the epiphytes in the canopy.

A walk down a western slope takes a hiker out of the forests and whistling winds and into an open woodland where trees shoot up to a high canopy. In the dry season, while the cloud forest drips in mist, the leeward slopes make do on sprinkles that blow down from the ridge. It's a tough, dry world for the epiphytes; here they thin out to a scattering. But here the birds and animals abound. From a

A raindrop taps a puffball—and out shoots a swirl of spores (opposite, left) to spread this fungus over the forest floor. Another fungus opens tiny umbrellas as its unseen tendrils weave through a fallen leaf. Both break down forest litter; the nutrients they recycle feed myriad plants and creatures in a complex web of life.

A weevil patrols a living leaf (opposite, upper) that may be its next meal. Jaws at the tip of its snout chew into leaves; females also gnaw holes for eggs.

A crab spider waits for prey on a shrub called hot lips (left, lower)—and may wait in vain, for butterflies will not seek this bud's nectar until it opens. The red "lips" are not petals but modified leaves called bracts.

Above it all, a two-toed sloth hangs lazily from a limb. Lethargic vegetarians, sloths are so adapted to treetop life that they can barely drag themselves along when on the ground. But they seldom need to, as they climb down to defecate only about once a week.

Biologist William Haber studies a butterfly under the gaze of his adopted Costa Rican daughter Marcela. Aided by National Geographic funds, Haber has found new species among the 500 he has identified at Monteverde. Half live in or near the reserve; the rest pass through on migration between lowland habitats. Monteverde is protected, but many distant habitats are not; thus humans who alter a habitat far from the reserve can skew the balance of wildlife within.

With a packful—and a mouthful—of specimens, botanist Nalini Nadkarni drops from the treetops. Her studies of the cloud forest canopy, funded in part by National Geographic, show epiphytes as prime gatherers of light, water, and nutrients for the whole forest ecosystem. A fern, a vine-like aroid, and a coating of moss burgeon on a tree trunk (lower right), growing, as the name epiphyte implies, "upon a plant," but taking their life from the air.

thicket comes the droll fluting of the elusive rufous-and-white wren, low-pitched as a human whistle. Chips fly as a golden-olive woodpecker hammers a stump in search of insects, both bird and bug helping to put the tree's nutrients back into the energy cycle.

Here come the howler monkeys, a troop of ten, scampering, snatching fruits and leaves, swelling their throats like bagpipes as they fill the air for half a mile around with their hoots. Here too are the sloths seldom seen on the ridge—and not often here, for their legendary lethargy is part of their camouflage. So is the algae that greens their fur in the wet months. A jaguar or eagle might look right at a sloth in a tree and not see it, hanging by its claws, looking like a bag of rags, viewing drowsily a world turned upside down.

The Quakers came seeking peace; now the scientists come seeking knowledge. In the reserve's dark crypts and sunlit eaves they pore over a rich catalog of life. Ferns as tall as trees. Ants that snip leaves into confetti and lug them to underground chambers, then feed on the fungus that sprouts as the bits decompose. Hummingbirds with names like green-crowned brilliant and purple-throated mountain gem, each with a bill tailored to the shape of the blossoms it probes. As each sips nectar, it pays its bar bill by picking up a dusting of pollen to deliver to the next blossom.

By such wondrous partnerships do bees, fruit-eating bats, and even mice serve as pollinators in the forests of Monteverde. Some fig varieties produce a round, hollow fruiting body with a small hole just big enough for the right pollinator; into the hole crawls a wasp, to find tiny blossoms wall-to-wall within.

Tourists come up the mountain too—seeking the quetzal. They greet each other with a standard query: "Do you bird?" Most of them do. Lugging binoculars, they trudge all day for a glimpse of a broad-billed motmot or tawny-throated leaftosser. In summer they listen for hours to the anvil chorus of the three-wattled bellbirds; young males have to practice the call diligently to perfect that ringing, metallic *bong!* But the great prize is the green, white, and scarlet bird many say is the most beautiful in the Americas—the resplendent quetzal. A glimpse is all it takes to know why the Aztecs and the Maya revered this bird and let only nobles wear its yard-long tail plumes of iridescent emerald.

Yes, I bird. By a laurel tree I watch a quetzal pluck fruits and gulp them whole. Nearby I find a thumb-size laurel nut, smooth as varnish, regurgitated by a quetzal after the pulp was digested. Thus the tree bribes the bird into spreading its seeds. It even regulates the bird's breeding, for in unusually dry seasons the stunted fruits do not give the quetzal the fat reserves needed for egg laying.

Along the Sendero Brillante I admire an impatiens in bloom. Suddenly a large animal thrashes in the thicket at trailside. *El tigre* hunts here, I have been warned—the jaguar. Too late to run; a huge beast explodes from the brush and flops into a puddle at my feet.

"Hullo, old chap!" the beast says with an English accent. "I just saw a wrenthrush. Bloody elusive; been trying to get close enough for four days. I say, do you bird?"

On my last day in Monteverde, Nalini takes me into a fairy tale. A few decades ago an amazing plant called a strangler fig began its life among the epiphytes high in a forest giant. It sent runners down the trunk, slowly caging the tree in a thickening braid of vines. The runners took root, fused together; the host tree strangled and rotted away. Now the fig stands alone, a latticed chimney with a hollow heart nearly a yard across.

Up the inside of the chimney we climb. Sixty feet up we crawl out on a limb of the fig. Again I am among old friends: fern, begonia, philodendron—and sudden mist. One does not come to Monteverde without a poncho; I huddle under mine and shed the windblown shower. And all around me the plants of the canopy drink it in, first in line for the moisture and nutrients that sustain life from canopy to ground in a forest hung in the clouds.

By David F. Robinson
Photographs by William E. Thompson

The Khyber Pass winds for 33 miles through Pakistan's Safed Koh Range.

HIGH FRONTIERS

George F. Mobley, National Geographic Photographer

Mountains divide us, hindering travel and trade, forming boundaries between nations. But such barrier regions may also become the prize in a border dispute, the frontier for an expanding—or invading—nation. The Khyber Pass, piercing the range between modern Pakistan and Afghanistan, led fifth-century Persian armies into India. Soldiers still guard this strategic route.

The claims of distant capitals may mean little to the people who dwell in a border area. Free-spirited highlanders rule in the rugged Tatras that divide Poland and Czechoslovakia. The mountains of China's Xinjiang region on the Soviet border shelter people who follow their own proud traditions. Serving as buffer zones, such regions help ease political tension.

Geology may attract settlers even as it hinders them. Rich ores in the rugged San Juans of Colorado brought eager miners, whose camps became frontier outposts.

SAN JUANS

Million-Dollar Mountains

Winter is the longest season in these San Juan Mountains of southwestern Colorado, six long months of magic and desolation like no other season, no other place I know. I came here first one February weekend ten years ago, and stayed. Got a crick in my neck staring up at snow-draped summits trying to puncture a cobalt sky; grew alarmed, then fascinated, finally bored with watching powder-snow avalanches cascade down shadowy north faces; finished the day with a lump in my throat as the last alpenglow turned frozen waterfalls into glowing red organ pipes, high snowfields into mauve drapes over storybook mountain skeletons. This is home, I told myself, after a lifelong love affair with mountains the world over—the San Juans are my mountains.

I was right. These peaks of the Colorado Rockies were even more special than I'd thought: jagged, pointed, abrupt, the sort of peaks a slightly mad art director might have dreamed up for a 1930s alpine adventure film. Much of the San Juan country is isolated, remote, a hard day's drive from almost anywhere outside. Yet, the mountains are also strangely humanized by small towns left over from the boom days of hard-rock mining. And they are accessible in a way so many of our great mountain sites, fenced and protected as national parks, are not.

White men got here in the 1870s—not settlers, but miners swept up in a feverish rush to find silver and gold. When the dust finally settled, the San Juans were no longer virgin mountains. Today there's much wildness,

Red Mountain No. 1 glows with oxidized minerals against the Colorado sky.

118

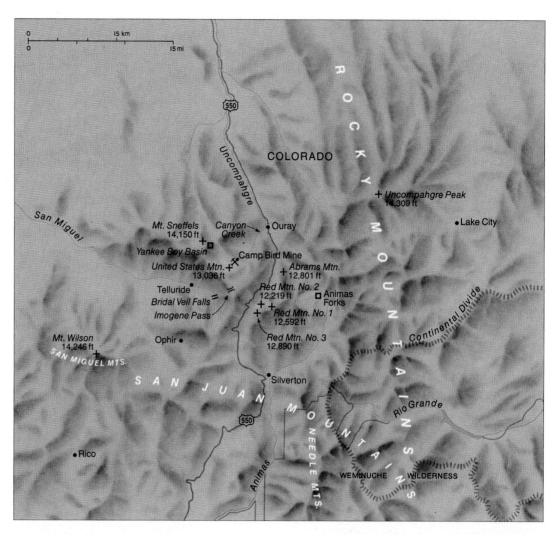

Fire and ice shaped the rugged, tightly clustered ranges of the San Juan Mountains in the southern Rockies. Titanic eruptions beginning about 35 million years ago piled slag and debris a mile high across a landscape of ragged, folded rock. Suddenly emptied magma chambers collapsed, creating enormous basins such as those at Silverton and Ouray. Subsequent upheavals injected the broken rock with gold, silver, and other minerals that would one day attract prospectors and miners. Glaciers scoured valleys and chiseled peaks, exposing some of the mineral deposits and leaving deeply scarred canyons and precipitous slopes prized by today's skiers and sightseers.

very little wilderness, in this range. Funky, old-fashioned San Juan communities maintain an uneasy coexistence with the most spectacular landscape in Colorado—a truce, an experiment to see whether so much grandeur can survive outside the confines of a national park. For better or worse these are populated, inhabited mountains—and most of the inhabitants are ghosts.

Winter is a good season for ghosts in the San Juans. Towns like Ouray become almost ghost towns. Standing in the middle of Main Street and looking up at the 2,000-foot-high snow-plastered cliffs, I try to people this landscape with the thousands of miners who swarmed over it at the turn of the century.

Try and fail.

It doesn't seem possible that people really lived up here all winter long in clapboard bunkhouses beneath giant drifts, mining, drilling, and blasting under such menacing slopes. It wasn't possible, really. Time and again avalanches would wipe out mills, supply trains, miners' cabins, and the miners themselves—lots of miners. Greed and gravity, a deadly combination in mountains this mean. But the mining never stopped, summer or winter, until the great easily exploitable ore bodies began to peter out in the early part of this century.

These San Juan valleys are choked with mining history—an awful lot of history piled up in such a short, desperate span of time. Half the towns are gone now: Sneffels, Ironton, Tomboy, Red Mountain Town. Some, such as Ophir and Rico, are only a couple of blocks long today, and more than half empty. A handful survive pretty much intact: Ouray, Silverton, Telluride, and Lake City.

Ouray is the sleepy capital of these mountains. And like its namesake Ute chief, who presided over a long series of bloodless defeats with uncommon dignity, the town has lived through its own series of defeats, almost all in the form of mine and mill closures. Tucked into an immense alpine bowl, Ouray is at a cross section of geological chaos at the head of the Uncompahgre River. It's a dollhouse town with turn-of-the-century cast-iron false fronts and baroque brickwork. In summer maybe as many as 1,500 residents, in winter barely 700. In winter many storefronts are shuttered, half the motels closed, sidewalks slippery with ice. The wind unfurls long snowscarves from the ridgelines above town, and there are almost no visitors to look up and admire them.

Winter and summer alike, the great Beaumont Hotel dominates the upper end of Main Street, boarded up for the last 20 years, brick cornices crumbling, mansard roof slowly collapsing. In front of the Beaumont it takes no imagination at all to hear a different class of ghosts partying behind the plywood-covered windows: sporting girls laughing, mine promoters romancing East Coast investors, crystal glasses shattering like icicles. The Italian miners who lived in a ghetto below the north end of Main Street never came here. The Swedes living up around Cascade Falls never came here. Now no one comes.

In the beautifully kept-up front parlor of a Victorian house on Fifth Street, admiring the hand-carved woodwork, the oak-and-tile

Paul Chesley

mantelpiece, the stained glass, I ask 88-year-old Frank Massard what folks do in Ouray in winter. "Mostly," he smiles back, "mostly we do without."

Frank and his partner, Albert Schneider, retired owners of the Post Office Drug Store, are among the lucky ones. They survived the heyday of San Juan mining by not working in the mines. Albert did work one all-night shift, came out in the morning, and told his friend, "I do believe it's deep enough; I'm not going back in there." The two of them wound up selling cough medicine to the young foreign miners who were dying of "miner's con" (consumption) from the dust of the "dry" drilling machines that were replacing slow hand drilling in the San Juan camps. Technological progress killed a lot of miners here. Did they know how dangerous it was? "Some did," Frank (Continued on page 124)

An old-time steam engine conjures clouds of nostalgia as it pokes through a midwinter blizzard in the San Juan Mountains. Its summertime run between Silverton and Durango —and shorter winter excursions—attracts more than 150,000 riders a year. Rails set only three feet apart, and lightweight rolling stock, linked many Rocky Mountain communities during mining's turn-of-the-century heyday. Rugged terrain made narrow-gauge routes easier and cheaper to build and maintain than standard-gauge rail lines.

allows, "but they wanted a job that bad. They would put up with anything."

Another survivor, white-haired Julius Sonza, born in Ouray on the Fourth of July 1897, painted me a dustier, deadlier picture: "I was mucking behind a dry machine at the Revenue. It was terrible. You had to take a wooden matchstick to dig the packed dust out of your ears and nostrils. Lucky I didn't die of it. A lot of my friends did."

Of another Ouray friend, Mel Griffiths, I ask: "Do you think those old-time miners ever really saw the mountains around them? Did they ever see any of this beauty?"

An uncomfortable pause; an uncomfortable answer: "No, most of them never really did. It was dig, dig, destroy, destroy. Striking it rich was all they really cared about."

Few ever did, though.

San Juan winter is a good season for memories, even uncomfortable memories. Snow piling up ten, twelve feet deep in the high basins. Avalanches poised, then releasing, mostly out of sight and far away—watched only by the restless ghosts of those who never struck it rich.

Spring sneaks up these mountain flanks one day, one contour line at a time. The San Juans wake up, foot by vertical foot. The snowpack changes, settles, sighs. In early May avalanche season is over and you can venture into high country on skis.

My wife, Linda, and I are standing on top of 13,114-foot Imogene Pass, out of slopes to climb and out of breath. Off to one side a scrappy-looking stone hut hunches under a snowdrift, all that's left of "Fort Peabody," where National Guard troops manned machine guns during the miners' strikes in 1903. Martial law as an early instrument of mine management. Long-gone scandals . . . tough times and tough men. Many of the leaders of the American trade union movement were forged in these San Juan labor troubles. And now we sit on this windswept ridge in our down jackets and daydream. Times change, we tell ourselves, but mountains don't . . . at least not too much.

A cherished memory: Skiborne, we lifted into the air off a gentle cornice and landed in a long, swooping turn. Edges bit, skis responded, senses vibrated. Three thousand vertical feet of rolling snowforms glided by beneath our skis: steep chutes, wide basins, forest glades, all the way down to Camp Bird Mine without a single other ski track. This was my own private San Juan gold mine.

On our way we skied past cliffs, skirted drop-offs, twined figure-eights down open bowls. At 11,400 feet we wove through ruins of the old (but now rebuilding) Camp Bird Level Three—rusted roofing, crazily tilted power poles. We spotted camp robbers—gray jays—perched on a broken gable, spring's first invaders. We contoured under the east face of United States Mountain, slid over 50-foot-deep avalanche debris, dove down a shortcut road, and wove into Camp Bird.

Compared with the snow-covered high country, this mine—one of the last operating mines in the area—looked like a war zone. Heaps of broken pipes and rusting machinery, the dead gray terraces of the tailings ponds. The snow here was thin and patchy, disappearing fast as spring climbed the narrow canyon walls. In a few more feet we were walking again, skis on our backs, down to Ouray, down through weeks of time, down from late winter into early summer.

Now, in this spring, we spot the first aspen leaves—buds really—tightly rolled, waxy, a translucent chartreuse against white trunks, so bright it almost hurts. In squishy hollows beside the dirt road, marsh marigolds are greening, and in another mile—there they are—the first flowers, white brush strokes in a dark green swamp. The slate gray canyon walls are hung with green moss, seeps, springs, and waterfalls. Canyon Creek roars along beside us, swollen with snowmelt as we walk all the way down into summer.

Summer in these San Juan mountain towns isn't measured by sunshine alone, but by cars parked on Main Street, by cash registers registering cash, by tourists in T-shirts and jeep jams on all the popular four-wheel

Memories of bonanza times linger in faded grandeur in and around Ouray. A crew still works the Camp Bird gold mine—a claim that yielded more than 26 million dollars around the turn of the century and may again approach boom. Local archivist Ruth Gregory holds a photographic glass plate that preserves the image of Ouray's town hall, destroyed by fire in 1950. An elegant Victorian house recalls bygone opulence. At Animas Forks, a ghost town nearby, houses in forlorn array hark back to the early 1900s, when the town prospered as a mine railhead.

roads, by afternoon thundershowers regular as clockwork, and by rogue rainbows that sneak over the peaks and grab you when you least expect it.

Ouray comes back to life, the retired folks and summer people arrive and unshutter their windows, the trailer court fills up, campers and mobile homes cruise through town. Once more Ouray looks like—and for four months becomes—a tourist mecca complete with rubber tomahawks and purple turkey feathers. Tourists and tourist dollars flow back into the San Juans with the regularity of swallows returning to Capistrano.

"Hell, tourism isn't the answer," growls Al Fedel, owner of a filling station in Ouray, between pumping gas for the very tourists who give him such mixed emotions. Talking to Al about mining is another story. He pulls out photos of his old drilling partners and tells me how they double-jacked their way to first place in hard-rock mining contests around the state, how important it was to sharpen your own "steels," how hard-rock miners are a different breed altogether. When Al talks about mining as the only real life for Ouray, he's speaking from the heart, from the heart of a town gripped by ghosts.

Tourism may or may not be the answer for these tiny San Juan communities, but everyone knows what the problem is—survival, making enough money to keep a family, a town, a way of life alive. In 1985 Ouray had one of the highest unemployment rates in Colorado. The people who live here can't eat the beauty that surrounds them.

Old-timers shake their heads when they talk about Telluride, the only mining town in the San Juans that has turned its back on its mining past and wholeheartedly embraced a tourist economy—ski resort in winter, festivals in summer. "You Telluride people," I hear over and over when folks in Ouray and Silverton learn where I live, "you Telluride people drove mining out; you made the Idarado Mill close down with all that ecological bull." They forget that ore prices have been falling and costs rising for years, that the

mining industry is on the ropes everywhere, not just in the San Juans.

"Mining has always been cyclical, a boom-and-bust industry," says a company official who, in 1984, had to lay off the last 40 miners at the Revenue/Virginius property. Everyone in Ouray will tell you the same story, but nobody wants to admit that this cyclical pattern has been a steady downhill slide—each boom smaller than the last, each bust bigger, each time a mine reopens, fewer jobs. How, I wonder, can the mining life have such a grip on this town when it was never more than a brutal, dangerous job?

The official gives me the perfect metaphor when he explains the geology of the Red Mountains, bright crimson landmarks between Ouray and Silverton: Their famous red color comes in part from oxidizing pyrite. These camelback peaks are giant heaps of rusted fool's gold!

The word "heap" has an ominous significance. The last gasp of a mining industry hell-bent on extracting the remaining gold from these mountains is a new process called cyanide heap leaching. Two experimental projects are under way in the San Juans, at Red Mountain and Summitville. Instead of following veins under the mountains, the new miners scrape away whole hillsides, extracting gold from even the lowest grade ore in great outdoor chemical ponds. These are not tough, hard-rock heroes; they are heavy-machine operators. If heap leaching proves economically viable, I can't imagine how the scenery of Colorado's most magical mountains can be preserved from power shovel and 'dozer. A depressing thought, and it dogs me through these summertime mountains.

By mid-July the alpine meadows are a crazy electric green, the mountain air soft and warm. High time to get into the high country.

Every summer I return like a pilgrim to Yankee Boy Basin, a slant-sided alpine valley nestled under the cliffs of 14,150-foot Mount Sneffels, only an hour's drive from Ouray. This tiny valley must be the mountain wildflower capital   *(Continued on page 133)*

A pioneering powerhouse nestles above the lip of Bridal Veil Falls near Telluride. Now in ruins, the plant was built in 1904 as an experiment to bring cheap alternating current to the Smuggler Union Mine nearby. Abundant water for power in these mountains prompted the boast that Telluride— electrified since 1891—was the world's best-lighted town.
Paul Chesley

Pages 128-129: The dazzle of a golden afternoon embowers a copse of quaking aspens near Telluride. The slightest breeze sets these leaves astir—delighting the ear as well as the eye. Stems set perpendicular to the leaf plane account for the aspen's ability to quiver.

Pages 130-131: Ajax Peak at the edge of Telluride unlimbers a snowy punch triggered by helicopter-borne explosives. Avalanche-control measures such as this are a part of winter life in the San Juans and help reduce the risk of disaster to miners, skiers, and motorists.
Bill Ellzey

Mecca to a swelling throng of outdoor enthusiasts, the San Juans offer a variety of activities, from dizzying cliff rides in the mountains around Ouray to balloon rallies and film festivals in Telluride. Mostly gone now are the hard-rock miners who eked a precarious living from these rugged hills. In their place have come droves of modern-day cyclists, skiers, hikers, and vacationers, who here find challenge for the body and sustenance for the soul.

of the world. For days on end, cameras in hand, Linda and I walk wide-eyed through this impossible landscape. Purple columbines first and foremost, thousands and thousands of them, knee-deep, waist-deep, a magic carpet, bigger and brighter than flowers have a right to be. Wine-dark pentstemon shadows. Impenetrable thickets of shoulder-high blue larkspur and violet monkshood. Endless variations of red, orange, and crimson paintbrushes. Pink moss campion and sky-blue sky pilots lording it over Yankee Boy Basin from the highest crags. In these mountains the flowers pursue you all the way to the summits of the fourteeners. And right in the middle of this tone poem of alpine colors, a bulldozer steadily gouges out a new road to an old mine that someone wants to rework. It's no use reminding myself that miners are an endangered species; I don't really care. Here the ghosts are too close, too greedy.

Autumn falls like fire onto these high, hard hills. Even the first dusting of snow can't retard the blazing aspens, the cottonwood coals glowing in creek beds, incendiary canyons of blast-furnace gold. Every year I think: This is it, these colors can't get any brighter, any richer, any deeper. They always do.

San Juan September burns slowly into October. Deer and elk drift downhill. The air is full of leaves, but stubbornly, impossibly, the last aspens keep turning. Winter already has the high basins in a hammerlock, and still the long flames of orange aspens lick their way to the edge of this new white.

And while they burn and glow and shimmer through the last autumn days, all the unanswered questions, all the contradictions of life in the San Juans are laid briefly to rest. Mining? Tourism? The dead end of history and the discomfort of the future don't seem to matter. Nothing matters except this final blaze of color. Everyone is moved, old-timer and tourist, miner and real estate developer. Everyone is speechless. Even the ghosts.

By Lito Tejada-Flores
Photographs by David Hiser

South of the Clouds

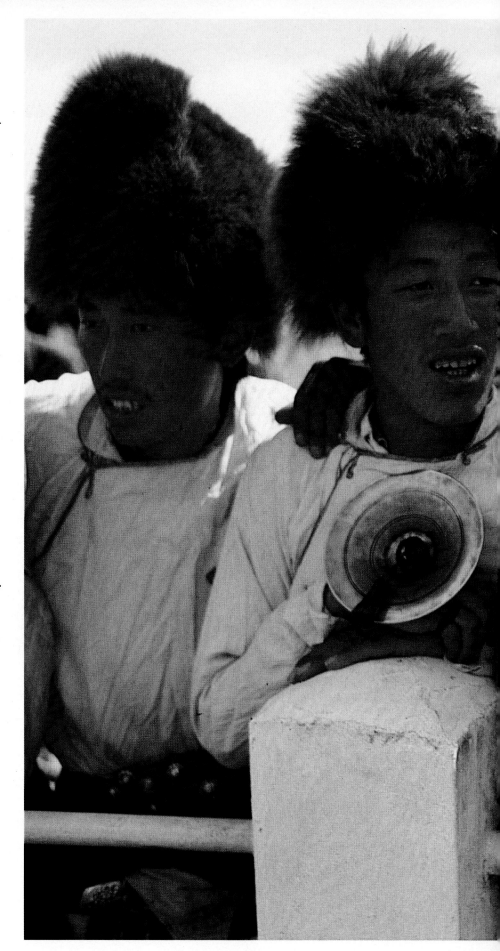

They come jostling and shouting in Day-Glo headdresses, high boots and sheepskins. Tribes with names such as Naxi, Bai, Lisu, Pumi, and Yi converge on the ancient gray town of Dali in Yunnan, China's southwestern border province. It is the Third Month Fair, an annual week-long gala of games, trading, and horse racing that has drawn mountain folk of this region together for over a thousand years.

I stand enthralled at one of Dali's towered stone gateways—remnants of the old city wall—as men and women, horses, baskets, banners, and carts crush through. Dali's human population of 11,000 has swollen tenfold and its livestock population fiftyfold. Crowds push between avenues of stalls in a babble of bargaining for radios, cloth, harnesses, bells, Western suits, umbrellas, and a hundred other wares. Frantic drumbeats part the throng as a swaybacked, two-man dragon sashays past with a family of acrobat-clowns.

"Twenty-one prefectures and autonomous counties greet our eyes!" exclaims one of the local organizers at the pageant-filled opening ceremony on the racetrack, as he expands a chest covered with official plastic badges. I recognize the different groups in the crowd only by the garb of the women. Brightest hued are the Bai women, streaming in from nearby villages. When not on parade, all men except for the Tibetans seem to dress alike in Chinese cotton jackets and caps.

Horse-loving Tibetans crowd the racetrack at an annual fair in Dali, China.

136

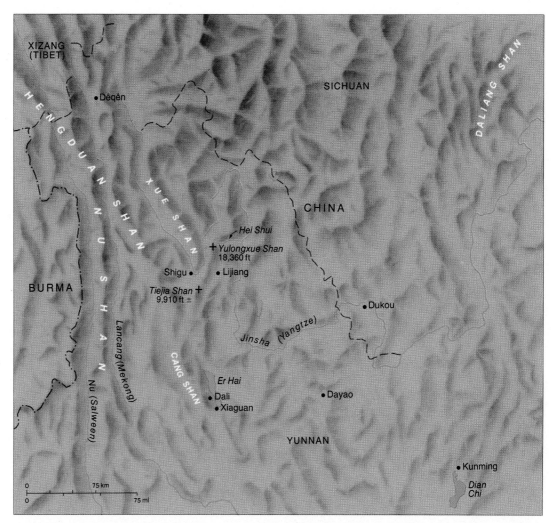

Yunnan is a geological offshoot of Tibet, whose rising tableland spills southeastward, creating a plateau over a mile high in eastern Yunnan. In the west, towering ranges fan south from Tibet's border, channeling some of southern Asia's greatest rivers, including the Yangtze. The 18,360-foot summit of Yulongxue Shan—Jade Dragon Mountain—marks the limit of the cloud-wreathed giants. The Cang Shan—Azure Mountains —reach only 13,000 feet.

South of the clouds—as Yunnan's name translates—dwell some of China's most diverse ethnic groups, among them the Bai, the Naxi, and the Yi. Their ancient cultures are slowly yielding to modernization by China's Han majority.

Dali is the ancestral home of the Bai. Since antiquity the town has linked the mountain fastness of the eastern Himalayas on Tibet's border with China's busy lowlands. Twelve hundred years ago it was the capital of a large kingdom called Nanzhao, which prospered through strategic alliances with its clashing neighbors, China and Tibet. Kublai Khan captured Dali in 1253, making it an outpost of China, but it remained a valuable junction.

Today jaunty Tibetans down from remote Dêqên, their fleece-lined coats flung off one shoulder, dominate the market of traditional medicine at the fair. No orderly rows of stalls here. Roots, twigs, dried plants, seeds, and fungi spill from sacks and baskets. By the time they reach Hong Kong, prepared and packaged into a thousand remedies, their value will have soared. I am saddened by shriveled bears' paws, desiccated snakes, antelope horns, and skins of snow leopard and pangolin, a scaly anteater. Alas, many Himalayan animals are being speeded into extinction because of the belief in their medicinal value.

Foreign faces were still a rarity in China's border provinces when I taught English at

Jodi Cobb, National Geographic Photographer

Yunnan University in Kunming from 1979 to 1982. Returning now to Yunnan Province after three years back home in the West, I find many changes. The Chinese authorities are promoting tourism and have opened Dali to foreign travelers. The Third Month Fair gives visitors a rare chance to see some of the colorful local groups. Twenty-three of China's fifty-five national minorities dwell in Yunnan, all with distinctive languages and cultures. Except for the fair, many of them rarely travel outside their mountain homes in sensitive border areas barred to foreigners.

No longer as free as in my teaching days, I am required to take along an official guide, but he turns out to be one of my old students. His classroom name had been Ernest—for Hemingway and for his own earnestness.

"We will be late for the horse races," calls Ernest, beckoning me up a slippery bank to bypass the crush. But we needn't risk our necks sprinting through the mooing, bleating, grunting, squealing livestock bazaar, because nothing starts on time. The sandy track is being used for a footrace, while some boys set up crossbow targets.

The small, strong horses finally arrive. Some are resplendent in silver ornaments and pom-poms, their wooden saddles jingling with bells. Others are sleekly bare. By twos and threes, twice around the track, riders compete furiously to the yells of onlookers, for a winning horse can be sold for 1,500 yuan—roughly equivalent to $500. Riders fall off. Some horses don't start, and others go racing off in the wrong direction. The crowd cheers anyhow.

An elderly Bai farmer beside me says this year's is the biggest, most elaborate fair he can remember, and he repeats one word emphatically. Ernest racks his brains for the right translation. "Sumptuous," he says.

One day Ernest and I took a boat trip on Dali's ear-shaped lake, Er Hai. It lay serene and unpolluted, cupped between mountains whose only scars were marble quarries above Dali. The western shore sloped gently up to the Cang Shan, its black soil sprouting with

Buddhist temple pagodas, built near Dali more than a thousand years ago, stand out vividly against the blue Cang Shan. The stone-and-brick towers, restored by Chinese emperors after earthquake damage in 1514, were renovated again in the late 1970s.

Buddhism spread to China from India by the end of the first century A.D. In Yunnan, as elsewhere, it blended with a variety of religious beliefs held by the local people.

rice, watered by mountain streams. Bumper crops of opium—sown each winter before the Chinese government suppressed the trade in the 1930s—were nearly forgotten. Across the lake, bare red cliffs rose abruptly beyond the water's edge, with fishing villages clinging precariously to their feet.

Square-ended wooden boats with converted tractor engines putt-putted through our wake. Some were draped with fishing nets. Others carried bricks, lumber, and cement blocks to building sites. An old Bai woman in a bright red bodice and tasseled hat sat blithely on the tiller of her 30-foot boat, maneuvering it on her own toward port. Bai villagers, closer than their mountain neighbors to the Chinese mainstream, have adapted to a variety of modern opportunities, and boat owners now match farmers in prosperity.

"Bai means 'white'," explained Li Po, our genial skipper, scraping fish scales off his brown hands as he prepared lunch.

"Why?" I asked.

His look implied that foreigners were dense. "Because we 'speak white.' Our women always wear something white and, well, we like white." A broad gesture proclaimed the matter to be self-evident.

The term, possibly of legendary origin, refers as much to language differences as to actual color associations. By "speaking white," the Bai mean that they use the Bai language rather than "speaking Han"—the language of China's national majority. The Bai and Pumi, who dwell south of Tiejia Shan—Iron Armor Mountain—call themselves "white," love bright colors, and keep white sheep and goats. The groups beyond Iron Armor—Naxi, Tibetans, Yi, and others—are said to favor black. Women's costumes are often black; so are their animals. Most of the people's names derive from roots meaning "black."

As we drove north from Dali, I took a good look at people along the roadside heading home from the fair. True, the costumes of "black" tribes looked sober compared to the incandescent Bai; but black and white sheep trotted together in the same flock, and a

A modern Chinese cap contrasts with traditional Naxi dress and dwellings in a village below Jade Dragon Mountain.
"Oh! Glorious is the sacred mountain!" read a Naxi inscription of the 16th century. "It is covered with snow throughout the four seasons, and stands like a piece of jade."

Pages 140-141: Baby rides along papoose-style as Bai women kneel in an island temple on Er Hai—"ear lake." The temple venerates Guan Yin, Buddhist goddess of mercy, patroness of women and fishermen, whom the Bai regard as their special protector. The Bai mix Buddhism with ancestor worship and recognition of Taoist and local folk deities.

black-clad Tibetan rode a white pony that still sported its winner's flag.

On the long ascent up Iron Armor Mountain, seasons ran in reverse. Dali's ripe, golden wheat gave way to young, green crops, and sprouting rice disappeared. As we approached the pass, wild azaleas spread like pink snowdrifts under the pines, and other trees were still in bud. Ahead of us rose the snowy head of Yulongxue Shan—Jade Dragon Mountain—18,360 feet high. Its 13 peaks piled aloft in a craggy mass, a sharp contrast to the long, looping skyline of the Cang Shan.

The little town of Shigu clutches a ledge above the Yangtze River's great bend. At its feet the river executes an abrupt U-turn and races away, gouging a cleft so narrow it is known as Tiger-Leap Gorge. Here the river is called Jinsha—"golden sands"—for the gold dust it brings from the Tibetan plateau.

The water, almost 50 feet deep at the bend, looks too swift to navigate. But crowning a high promontory is a monument of Dali marble that commemorates a momentous crossing here. In April 1936 a branch of Mao Zedong's Red Army reached Shigu on its grueling Long March, with the Nationalist Army close behind. In three unforgettable days and nights, the tough Naxi mountain men helped ferry 18,000 Red Army soldiers to safety by makeshift raft and riverboat.

The matriarchal Naxi originated in Tibet, migrating to Yunnan some 2,000 years ago. Their pictographic script is thought to have developed long before other minorities became literate. Until modern times the Naxi capital of Lijiang, some 20 miles east of Shigu, was the chief trading center between Tibet and southern China. Yak trains carried down Tibet's medicine and wool and trudged back to Lhasa with brick tea and Chinese goods purchased from the Naxi. At times a quarter of Lijiang's population was Tibetan.

Lijiang's bustling marketplace is run today by energetic Naxi women, tublike in their bulky, black-and-blue costumes with sheepskin capes. But the old ways are disappearing. Chinese workers' caps rather than black

Minority groups from every corner of Yunnan gather to see and be seen at the Third Month Fair in Dali. At the opening parade, a local sports group writhes through the motions of a dragon dance. Once considered a powerful water god, the bringer of spring rains, the dragon remains a good luck symbol to Chinese. So do bats, which Dai dancers represent in iridescent colors.

Bai women (lower, left) proclaim their unmarried status by the long tassels on their embroidered headdresses. Fur-capped Tibetans ride their sturdy ponies near Dali's south gate. China's officials, with an eye to tourism, encourage attendance by all of Yunnan's colorful national minorities.

Naxi bonnets now complete the women's outfits, and the Tibetans have left Lijiang. Trucks replace yaks, and Naxi traders are no longer needed as middlemen.

Old Lijiang, a mountain town of stone and tile laced with swift canals, adjoins New Lijiang, whose wide streets, apartment blocks, and department stores have clones in other towns throughout China.

In the suburbs, big sawmills do a thriving business. The practical Naxi, shorn of their role as traders, exploit their rich forest reserves for wood-hungry China's bottomless timber market. Power saws devoured forests indiscriminately until the government heeded the warnings of ecologists in 1983. Now officials enforce a reforestation program.

The mountains continue to nurture the Naxi, but the ancient mountain gods have loosened their grip. *Dongbas,* the Naxi sorcerers who held access to the spirit world, did not survive under Communism. Their store of Naxi folklore and history might have been lost but for a few Naxi scholars, such as Zhao Jin-xiu, who started a local museum in 1954. Mr. Zhao showed me dongba books written in an antique Naxi script that only dongbas could read. The spongy paper was made from a bark impervious to insects or fire. Thousands of volumes covered subjects ranging from exorcism to accounting.

Dongbas told how Tabu, the common Naxi ancestor, came from the sky and helped the people hatch from magic eggs. Tabu is still cherished in family shrines, along with the spirits of ancestors whom all Naxi honor privately in their homes.

The Naxi have traditionally mingled little with the shy Lisu to the east, skilled hunters with the crossbow, whom they considered wild people. And even less with the Yi.

There are 30 branches of Yi, fourth largest of China's 55 national minorities. In ancient times, groups fanned out from their ancestral home in Sichuan's Daliang Shan—Great Cool Mountains. They settled in other places and did well, even royally. Rulers of the Nanzhao Kingdom in the eighth and ninth centuries were said to be Yi. Wherever they went, the Yi acquired a reputation for bold independence. They clung to their own ways.

Those among Yunnan's peaks thrived as brigands. Riding out from mountain strongholds in the Jade Dragon, the aristocratic Black Yi lived by a code of chivalry and plunder. The low-caste White Yi lived in bondage under their protection. The White Yi farmed around their masters' mountain fortresses and served as their contact with the outside world, trading horses and opium for them. After the Communist revolution of 1949, the caste system among the Yi was abolished, and the Black Yi ruling class disappeared from the Jade Dragon. The White Yi continued to scratch out farms around their old haunts, out of sight except for occasional appearances in Lijiang's market—until Naxi loggers opened roads to their doorsteps.

With Mr. Zhao and Ernest, I drive across a barren, rock-strewn plain under the flank of the Jade Dragon. The road leads up and up past vistas of long, forested valleys with no sign of human habitation. We climb beyond the cascading Hei Shui—"black water river" —to a raw scar of earth 9,000 feet high, with the snow of the mountain above us. Naxi workmen are hewing beams by hand amid foundations for a forestry station. Only then do I see low, windowless dwellings hugging the mountainside. Rocks on their crudely shingled roofs blend with the landscape. Ragged children scramble to the roadside to stare. Women in flounced skirts and black, tentlike headdresses approach warily, grab as many children as they can hold, and retreat with faces averted. A man with a heavy, black, pleated cape and turban appears.

"He says you can visit the village," says Mr. Zhao. "Don't bring the camera—the women are afraid that it will give them diseases." It takes half an hour of persuasion by Mr. Zhao in their own language before the women reluctantly come out and pose. "These are *real* Yi," says Ernest. "They will never change." The villagers take no part in construction or forestry work, shunning contact with others.

Marble dust flies as a woman grinds a piece of dalishi—*Dali stone. The town has been famed since imperial times for its fine marble. Here quarrymen shape slabs on a Cang Shan mountainside. Factory workers then fashion them into vases and other works of art, such as this signed mountain landscape, found in the stone's natural markings.*

Pages 146-147: Er Hai spreads its sapphire waters at the foot of the Cang Shan. Residents of this Bai fishing village on the northeast shore grow rice in flooded paddies. Poor soil forces them to make their living mostly from the lake—by fishing, or perhaps by transporting building materials.

Rounding its great bend, the Yangtze turns sharply northeast toward Jade Dragon Mountain, then winds east across China. At this bend Naxi villagers, like the smiling mountain man holding a water pipe, helped ferry Red Army troops across the river during the Long March of 1936.

On the other side of the mountain, somberly dressed White Yi live much as they have for centuries in isolated farming villages (opposite); rocks secure their roof shingles. The White Yi woman puffing on her pipe shows more confidence than is usual for this shy, suspicious people, whose wild frontier world is ruled by the good and evil spirits of their animist religion.

The straggling village is about as minimal as a community can be, but there are endearing touches. Shelters for pigs and goats are made with care, small versions of their owners' homes. There is a sense of friendliness between man and beast, between the village and the mountain.

"The Yi will never change" stayed in my mind as we drove back to Lijiang. Unlike the adaptable Bai and the practical Naxi, they seem stuck fast in a vanishing world. Before long, forest roads and chain saws will destroy their world, serving the insatiable needs of a more advanced one. Would the White Yi go the way of the snow leopard and pangolin?

Over Lijiang's marketplace, clouds gathered. Rain soon followed. As I ducked into a doorway for shelter, an authoritative hand pulled me inside. Its owner, Long A-xian, beautiful and saucy in her old-style Naxi bonnet, was born near Tiger-Leap Gorge in 1905. "When I was 13, my father sold me for 50 silver coins and a pound of opium," she said matter-of-factly, settling comfortably on her stool as rain pounded the windowpanes.

A-xian had spunkily refused to marry her purchaser. "He was revolting," she confided. "No hair at all." But she remained as an unpaid servant in his family for years. At the ripe age of 24, she was sold in marriage to a wealthy trader, a widower in his 50s, and bore him 2 daughters. But his rapacious sister and older daughter laid claim to his property and made her life unbearable. "Twice I swallowed opium. I wanted to kill myself," said A-xian. But when her husband died, she outfought her in-laws and kept his house.

"And now?" I asked.

"Hard to believe," she replied. A-xian owns three market tables, which she rents out. Her daughters, with jobs and families of their own, drop in daily and provide for her needs. Her granddaughter, her pride and joy, attends college in Chengdu. "I hope I never die," said A-xian.

By Elisabeth B. Booz
Photographs by Thomas Nebbia

From relatives in the United States came fabric, beads, and sequins for these traditional costumes of the Polish Tatras.

A Highland Stronghold

He was a mountain man. And a survivor. Stanislaw Marusarz had been close to death at the hands of the Nazis once before. He'd escaped by diving through a window and, bleeding badly, walking 20 miles to a comrade's house.

Marusarz made several more trips as a courier through the high passes of the Tatras, spiriting arms, supplies, and messages across the frontier from southern Poland into Czechoslovakia and then to Hungary, a vital link between the Polish resistance and the West. But now, in June 1940, it seemed his luck had run out. The Gestapo jailed Marusarz, beat him, and sentenced him to death. He and 250 other prisoners were forced to dig their own graves.

Knowing they would soon be killed, Marusarz and his cellmates dismantled a table and used the planks to pry apart the bars on the window. One by one the men leapt 20 feet, landing on barbed wire. Sirens blared. The Germans began shooting. Marusarz kept running.

Marusarz symbolizes the physical courage and spiritual stamina of the *górale,* the highlanders of the Polish Tatras whose name comes from *góra,* or mountain. Vigorous and spirited and ready for anything, the górale tend to live beyond the law. Today they smuggle food, mountain-climbing equipment, and car parts from Czechoslovakia; during martial law in the

152

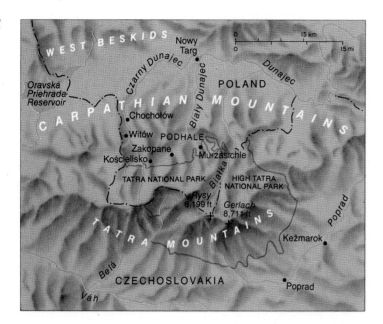

Curving in a gentle crescent from the Alps to the Balkans, the Carpathian range shoots up along the Polish-Czech frontier. Here in the Tatras— the highest peaks in the Carpathians—sedimentary rocks sheathe a core of granite and gneiss. During the last Ice Age, melting glaciers chiseled deep valleys and filled them with water. Streams born high in the Tatras feed Poland's most important river, the Vistula.

The Tatras divide Poland from Czechoslovakia, but folk art, songs and dances, costumes, and customs link the mountaineers. Though much of highland folk culture has vanished in Czechoslovakia, Poland's górale still cling to their free-spirited ways.

Zakopane, Poland's favorite mountain resort (opposite), gained renown as a health spa in the 1880s. Today more than two million holidaymakers come to the Tatras each year. But the pure air that first drew visitors now tastes of coal dust from stoves and furnaces.

early '80s, they spirited antigovernment activists out of Poland.

Historically, the górale have enjoyed a freedom not experienced by other Poles. In the 13th and 14th centuries, their ancestors roamed northwest along the Carpathian Mountains from the Balkan Peninsula, in search of pastures for their sheep. Feudalism never worked well in the Tatras because the górale rebelled or melted into the mountains whenever outsiders threatened. When Prussia, Russia, and Austria carved up Poland in the late 1700s, the Tatra region fell under the more tolerant Austrians. Many lowland Poles sought refuge here. Later, so did Lenin, on his way to Russia and revolution.

To the peasants who endured the severe climate, rocky soil, and trackless forests haunted by wolves and wildcats, Tatra originally meant "wasteland." But in a flat country that lay, temptingly, across the path of countless invaders, these rugged mountains have helped the górale hold to their cherished traditions. The empires that claimed in the past to rule Poland's frontier really only controlled the plains and one or two passes through the mountains, much like the northwest frontier of Pakistan. For a thousand years, until Nazi tanks roared into southern Poland, no war touched the Tatras.

In the 1880s Poland's writers, musicians, and artists "discovered" the Tatras and promoted them as the cradle of Poland, of Polishness—the least changed region in the country. One poet elevated the highlanders to the status of Homer's heroes. "Tradition is your dignity, your pride, your nobility, oh peasant son," extolled a novelist.

Many of today's górale raise

sheep and do a little farming, as much as the short summer and thin soil allow. Generations of shepherds have handed down stories, songs, and dances that keep góral traditions alive. One legend tells of Janosik, the Slavic version of Robin Hood. Betrayed by a woman, Janosik was hung by his rib, smoking a pipe while a fire burned at his feet. "Now that you've cooked me, eat me," he shouted. He died and the mountains cried, mourning the fallen hero.

The traditional world of the górale extends only two or three miles from home, a carriage ride away. Horses take the górale to church, to market, to christenings and weddings and funerals. Horse-drawn plows are cheaper and more practical than tractors, which would tear up the thin mountain soil.

Though time moves slowly in the Tatras, a fast-changing world is beginning to unravel centuries of tradition. Many highlanders commute to work in the mountain resort town of Zakopane or in factories near Nowy Targ. Young górale seek education and jobs elsewhere. Some work in America for a few years, then return with more money than if they'd labored in Poland all their lives.

Change is coming, but the Tatras—and the independent-minded górale who love them— endure. The highlanders tell of a scrawny góral dog who meets a well-fed Czech dog on the border. "Why are you coming to my country?" asks the Czech dog.

"To eat," replies the Polish dog. "And why are you crossing into my country?"

"So I can bark."

By Carol Bittig Lutyk
Photographs by John Eastcott
& Yva Momatiuk

153

Ribbonlike fields give each farmer equal access to sun and good soil but thwart modern technology.

Snow settles on the heavily wooded Tatras for more than 200 days each year.

Forged by an austere life and
tempered by an exhilaratingly
beautiful land, góral traditions
hold firm in a fast-changing
world. Houses and barns of
thick spruce logs—a woodcut-
ter's fantasy—dwarf a woman
scrubbing rugs. Steep roofs
shed snow; pegs, not nails, fas-
ten the log walls, which are
chinked with wood shavings.

Wood gives birth to music,
too. Spruce trees grow slowly
in the thin mountain soil, producing dense, resonant wood
prized for musical instruments.
An insatiable love for music
keeps górale feet flying. Two
days of dancing and feasting
will follow the wedding of the
couple at left. The bride pins
flowers to the groom's felt cloak
—a time-honored góral custom.

On the Northwest Frontier

We were standing with our backs to the fort, the colonel of the Chitral Scouts and I, watching sunset touch the Hindu Kush with rays of pure gold. The mountains were only a few miles away across our valley, which was turning a deep mauve in the shade, and just beyond the topmost ridge was Afghanistan, where there may have been much fighting (gunships versus guerrillas) that day. But on our side of the Pakistani frontier, night would be falling softly again, the loudest sound being that of the Chitral River down below the fort. We could hear it rushing along its rocky bed between the mountain walls, on its way toward Jalalabad and a junction with the Kabul River.

The colonel was Punjabi by birth, therefore a plainsman bred, but he had become enthralled by the hill country of his command. As we savored the late glowing light together, he said something, much more to himself than to me.

"... Though every prospect pleases, And only man is vile," he murmured, in a benediction on it all. A devout Muslim soldier quoting a fragment of a Christian hymn. It was improbable but entirely appropriate in that luminous place.

The Chitral District of Pakistan's North-West Frontier Province isn't quite on the roof of the world, but it's near enough, tucked up there just under the eaves. Only a little bigger than Connecticut, it is essentially a river

Glacier-clad Tirich Mir, the highest peak in the Hindu Kush, guards Pakistan's border with Afghanistan.

162

"In no other part of the world," wrote a British spy in the 1880s, *"is there found such lofty mountains within so confined a space."* Geologically young and still active, the Karakorams and neighboring Hindu Kush thrust aloft where the Indian subcontinent presses into Asia. Here stand some of the world's highest mountains, with 25 peaks over 25,000 feet.

At the crossroads where China, Russia, Afghanistan, and India converge, Pakistan's northwest frontier has been a pathway for invaders since 1500 B.C. In this remote mountain world lives an astonishing mix of people, from descendants of Alexander the Great's army to newly arrived Afghans fleeing Soviet invaders at home.

valley shaped like a boomerang, 220 miles long, held tightly within some of the mightiest mountains on Earth. The Hindu Kush curve along its western side until they run into the main Karakoram Range at the top. From the Hindu Kush drops the massive spur of the Hindu Raj, which barricades Chitral to the east. In that relatively small area there must be hundreds of sensational peaks. More than 40 are over 20,000 feet.

Almost wherever you are in Chitral, the grandest of them all looms like some overwhelming totem of the gods. Tirich Mir touches 25,230 feet, its ice cliffs dull or gleaming white according to the position of the sun, a spume of snow invariably flaring into the sky, blown from the summits by tempestuous winds. A local legend insists that the mountain is guarded by giant frogs, called *boguzai*, and by phantom maidens

who meet climbers with bowls of milk or blood; to drink the blood is surely to die. This daunting tale may partly explain why Tirich Mir was not climbed until 1950, when a party of Norwegians at last made it to the top.

The lower slopes of mountains in southern Chitral are generally a mixture of meadow and scree, clad patchily with forests of deodar, fir, spruce, pine, and oak. Most trees disappear in Chitral's arid north, with only occasional flourishes of birch and juniper, willow and poplar, walnut and plane. The tree line comes between 12,000 and 13,300 feet, and thereafter it is bare rock at the best of times, but for most of the year snow and ice, perpetually so in the case of the highest ground. It is an intimidating landscape, not one for those whose need is to be gentled through life. Even at the lowest altitudes the temperatures are generally fierce. Beside the

In a reckless free-for-all, polo players charge down Gilgit's long field to the cheers and jeers of male spectators. Mountain polo, northern Pakistan's favorite sport, hardly resembles the more genteel game played elsewhere in the world. Women, cloistered at home, can tell who's winning by listening to the pipe-and-drum band wailing a player's signature tune each time he scores. In bygone days the victors sometimes chopped off the losers' heads.

Pages 164-165: Supply-laden trucks grind and squeal over 10,230-foot Lawarai Pass, just north of the route traveled by Alexander the Great when he invaded India in the fourth century B.C. Light vehicles are often loaded with bags of wheat or other ballast to keep them from slipping over the edge as they tackle the 40 or so steep hairpin bends. Snow cuts off the pass in winter. From late spring until December, vehicles maneuver around landslides, avalanches, and fallen trees blocking the rutted dirt track.

Chitral River, at over 5,000 feet, it can register 110°F in July, and 20° six months later.

The contrast between the uplands and the extended valley of inhabited Chitral is dramatic in the five months of spring and summer. My own visit began at the end of May, and I found that, while everything above the valley was still magnificently bleak, down below all was fertile abundance. Orchards were everywhere, bearing peaches and apricots, mulberries and plums. Other crops were grown in small fields bound by dry-stone walls—wheat and barley and maize for the most part, sometimes rice.

Water there is in plenty, tumbling down the mountainsides, and every small community from one end of Chitral to the other has networked itself with irrigation ditches, the flow being carefully controlled by rudimentary sluices homemade from slabs of stone. The fruits are dried for winter eating, and nuts are picked. Beyond that and the other crops, there is the milk, wool, and meat from flocks of sheep and goats. At an ascetic level, Chitral is almost wholly self-contained.

No community is very big. Chitral Bazaar, the traditional center of the district, may not contain as many as 30,000 souls. It sprawls beside a bend in the river, which can be crossed there on two bridges. One is quite recent and a tidy piece of civil engineering; so was the other when it was suspended on hawsers from one bank to the other nearly a century ago, but now it is apt to sway unnervingly when a vehicle tries to squeeze across its narrow planks. Just upstream is the most conspicuous building in Chitral, the Shahi Mosque, whose large, dazzling white domes have been prettified with delicate patterns in blue, green, and red. When the muezzin

Vestiges of the British Empire linger as tartan-clad pipers of the Chitral Scouts play old Scottish airs at their headquarters in Drosh, only 16 miles from Afghanistan. Its tree-shaded green, Tudor-style officer's mess, silver butter dishes and saltcellars, walnut furniture—all seem more like England than a frontier outpost high in the Hindu Kush.

In 1903 sharpshooting tribesmen formed the Chitral Scouts to defend the northwest frontier against Russian and Afghan invaders. Today's Scouts still keep a sharp eye on the 26 passes between Chitral and Afghanistan. In recent years the men suffered casualties when Russia escalated air and artillery strikes inside Pakistan, probably to subvert local support of the Afghan guerrillas.

broadcasts the prayer times by loudspeaker from Shahi's minaret, his nasal chant skirls weirdly round the echo chamber created by the surrounding mountainsides. That sound in that place I shall never forget.

The main thoroughfare here is a long and dusty lane between two lines of open-fronted boxes which serve as shops. Though they seem pitifully understocked to Western eyes, there is nothing so ample for fifty miles or more in any direction—hence Chitral *Bazaar.* Along its line of shops, men squatted in the dust, gossiping, keeping an eye open for strangers, waiting for trade. One fellow, more ragged than the rest, crouched some distance from the others, stroking a mangy dog. From time to time, the man threw back his head and howled like a dog—though the animal itself never made a sound.

In villages elsewhere along the valley, no more than half a dozen such box shops line the main street. Above those dusty lanes everywhere rise the Chitrali homes, built of timber and rough stone, layered in terraces up the hillsides. Sometimes the ground on which they are built is so steep that the tightly packed earth roof of one house is the yard of the dwelling above. The walls are immensely thick, to retain warmth in winter, to repel heat in summer. Also as some kind of insurance if an earthquake should befall. Small tremors occur quite often here.

Within its tremendous ranges, Chitral is as isolated as any civilized community can now be on this Earth. Here is a long string of villages, most containing no more than a few thousand folk, snugged down along the boomerang shape of the valley floor.

There are many routes through those mountains known to people traveling on two feet or four, but otherwise there are but three ways to get in and out. One is by jeep across the 10,230-foot Lawarai Pass, Chitral's gateway to the south. Another is by similar rough-riding over the even higher (12,222 feet) Shandur Pass, which leads to Gilgit in the east. But neither of these passages is available between December and the following

168 May, when Chitral is locked in by one blizzard after another, a snowbound wilderness. Access then depends wholly on a resilient little Fokker Friendship of Pakistan International Airlines, which is supposed to fly up from Peshawar to the little landing strip at Chitral Bazaar daily throughout the year. It is a hazardous flight even at the height of summer, stormy weather often forcing the pilots to turn back over Lawarai. In winter Chitral is frequently cut off for weeks at a time. Sometimes things get so bad that the Pakistan Air Force has to make an emergency run with vital supplies.

There are about 200,000 people up there, all told, in what was once a princely state, semiautonomous right to the finish of British imperial rule (the Raj), its *mehtar* being awarded an 11-gun salute by grace and favor of the Raj, provided he didn't step too far out of line. This small deference, and the latitude allowed the ruler in ordering Chitral's internal affairs, was a measure of the strategic importance attached to the little state. A glance at the map shows why.

Chitral, quite simply, belongs to one of the world's historical frontiers. It is close to the area where, in the 19th century, three powerful empires converged: those of Queen Victoria, the Russian tsar, and the Manchu Dynasty of China. It lies beside the route that has been taken for 2,000 years and more by all who would pass from Central Asia to the Indian subcontinent, in peace or at war. When Alexander the Great with his Macedonians poured out of Bactria in 327 B.C., he took half his army over a pass below Lawarai and sent the rest over the more southerly Khyber Pass. And almost every century since then has seen some sort of incursion from the same direction across the northwest frontier.

For nearly as long, traders have dispatched their caravans of camel and yak over the mountain passes both ways, along one of the great commercial thoroughfares of the East. A branch of the famous Silk Road from China came by here on its way to Peshawar, descending from present-day Xinjiang across

Imprints of East and West bear witness to Chitral's variegated past. The strongest bond is not race or language but a common creed—Islam, borne by Turks and Afghans through the Hindu Kush. Muslims gather at Chitral's 50-year-old mosque on Fridays, their holy day. Women worship apart from men.

From ancient Persia came another trademark of the East—the omnipresent bazaar. Along Chitral's main street, shops sell everything from sizzling kabobs to sandals made of old tires, all coated with dust stirred up by passing traffic.

British spit and polish pervades Chitral Scout headquarters. Like the corkscrew-horned markhor, adopted as their insignia, the soldiers traverse their lofty realm with ease.

Pages 170-171: Poplars and willows capture the last glint of autumn, foreshadowing winter's descent on the Gilgit River. Snow and cold killed so many Indian slaves en route to Central Asia that these mountains earned the name Hindu Kush, or "Hindu killer."

Crowned with cowrie-shell headdresses, women of the Kalash tribe sidestep slowly to the sound of drum and flute, celebrating the autumn harvest. A young dancer (opposite) wears a cap garnished with fruit. Their distinctive dress, animistic religion, and customs reminiscent of pre-Christian Europe set these tall, fair people apart from their Muslim neighbors.

The Kalash raise goats and wine grapes in three remote valleys in the central Hindu Kush. Their tiny houses climb willy-nilly up slopes so sheer that the roof of one house becomes the threshing floor for the one above. The entire family—sometimes with a dozen or more members—cooks, eats, and sleeps in one room.

the rugged passes in the north of Chitral. 173
Marco Polo learned of lapis lazuli and ruby
mines in his traverse of Badakhshan, which
is not more than a few day's hard climb from
the fort where the colonel and I were spell-
bound by the setting sun.

The Chitral Scouts that my friend com-
manded were raised in 1903 precisely because the British wanted to guard all those
northwestern loopholes into India against
possible invaders—and in those days they
had the tsar mostly in mind, especially since
his Cossacks had crossed Chitral's boundaries 12 years before. Though the Raj in due
course ended, the Scouts soldiered on, and
they still perform the function they were originally intended for. A fort full of them is perpetually on guard beside the Baroghil Pass,
just in case Russians or anyone else hostile
should come through from the other side.
The full muster of Scouts amounts to 4,000
experts in mountain warfare, whose regimental pipe band wears the Royal Stuart tar-
tan on ceremonial occasions even now, and
whose officers' mess has affectionately retained photographs of the old British com-
manders on its walls. Crack marksmen all,
though they have lately suffered casualties at
the hands of the Russians.

There will scarcely be a male in all Chitral
who isn't deadly with a rifle before he has left
his teens. As soon as an infant boy can walk,
ballistics become an important part of his life.
Just about every field wall along the valley
seems to conceal its quota of youngsters lying
in ambush for birds, which they hit with depressing accuracy by firing stones from cata-
pults fashioned out of conveniently Y-shaped
saplings cut down to hand-size, the missile
propelled by elastic stretched across the
prongs of the Y. When arm muscles have
strengthened, stones (not arrows) are fired
from the double-stringed Chitrali bow, and
with this weapon large rodents or small game
a hundred yards away can at least be stunned
long enough for the hunter to rush up and
kill with the knife. The transition to firearms
soon after is a simple one.

174   No such excitements are in store for little girls. This is a rigorously Muslim society for the most part, whose adherents belong to either the Sunni or the Ismaili sect. Which means that the vast majority of Chitrali women live in purdah, swathed in the all-concealing burka on the infrequent occasions when they are permitted to travel away from the house, where they are licensed to be the dutiful wife and mother, nothing more. I have been told that many women arrange to be chaperoned to the medical dispensary in Chitral Bazaar not so much because they are ailing, but so that they may clap eyes—surreptitiously, through the facial slit in their garment—on a man outside their immediate family for a change.

The local mania for marksmanship explains the serious loss of wildlife in Chitral since the rifle made its appearance here, though in recent years the federal government has regulated hunting. All this hill country once crawled with several varieties of mountain sheep and goat, and their natural predators as well. The urial, a reddish brown sheep with a white neck and beard, is now almost extinct, as is the brown bear. Herdsmen used to shoot the mother bears and sell the cubs to traveling entertainers, who taught them to dance. Markhor are no longer to be seen much; this large mountain goat, most celebrated of the local ungulates, has spiraling horns, a small beard, and a neck ruff that in mature males often descends from the neck to the knees. The markhor's head was adopted by the Chitral Scouts as a regimental badge, and the only living beast I have seen is the one the Scouts keep as a mascot, an ill-tempered billy that may or may not answer to the name of Morarji.

Saddest decline of all has been that of the snow leopard, most beautiful of the big cats, whose fur of soft gray, paling to white, explains the determination with which it has been hunted for decades. It has been estimated that there were fewer than 250 of them in all the highlands of Pakistan back in the early 1970s. We shall be lucky if as many of them

On a precipitous mountainside in the Kagan Valley, stone-walled terraces hold back the precious soil, providing level areas for planting rice and wheat. Landslides are a constant threat to field and house. In a region devoid of heavy industry and large towns, the hardy inhabitants eke out a meager living. Whole villages close down in spring and move with their livestock to subalpine meadows. There they fish the streams for trout, introduced by the British in the 1920s.

Pages 176-177: "Goddess of the snows," 25,550-foot Rakaposhi reigns over the Hunza Valley, said to be the model for legendary Shangri-La. Once a major caravan stop on the Silk Road from China, this isolated realm is not the heaven on earth glorified by writers. Unsanitary conditions, poor diet, and inadequate medical care lead to ravaging diseases and death, especially among infants.

are with us still. Near the polo field at Chitral Bazaar, a tin plate tacked onto a fence post bears a picture of the cat, and the words in two languages: "Snow leopard. Please do no kill me. I am protected animal." Someone has punctured the notice with bullet holes.

Polo demonstrates the more acceptable face of Chitral's masculinity. The game was first played in this part of the world, and not even hunting is more of a local obsession. When Chitral Bazaar played Gilgit, they did so on top of the Shandur Pass, because it is the only level ground approximately equidistant between the two towns; at over 12,000 feet, it is also the highest polo ground in the world. Crowds of supporters from both sides of the Hindu Raj made the occasion their annual holiday, as they needed to, given the time it took them and the players to travel to the game. The Chitralis had a four-day ride each way through the mountains on horseback, the Gilgitis six.

The smallest village, whose only patch of open ground may be the dusty surface that passes for a main street, will play its chukkers right there. In Chitral Bazaar, though, they have a Yankee Stadium of a field, with a tiny grandstand where dignitaries can sit, proper goalposts, and an enclosure where bandsmen perform throughout the game on reed instruments (*surnai*) and drums (*dol*). Every polo player has his own signature tune, and the moment he scores or rides especially well, the bandsmen switch from the last number and let his tune rip.

And it is a wild, wild game of polo they play up there, not at all the genteel sport we are accustomed to in the West. Helmets are spurned in favor of the frontier's customary headgear for men, the woolen beret resembling a Tudor cap, which Chitralis call *pakhol*. No pony has its fetlocks bandaged, and most are bleeding when time is called. The horsemanship is superb. To watch a Chitrali in full flight for goal, his stick pointing straight forward like a leveled lance, the rest of the riders charging in a cloud of dust on either side of him, is to have an inkling of what

Rhythms unchanged for centuries mark the daily round of life in the Swat Valley. To Bahrain's bazaar come men from town and countryside, mingling and haggling in the tiny shops, sipping sweet milk tea, gossiping, promenading. Artisans like this silversmith (above) produce jewelry that echoes Swat's Buddhist past, as do the decorative motifs on many houses. Buddhists settled here in the second century B.C., leaving behind elegant sculptures and 1,400 monasteries. In the eighth century A.D., Hinduism took hold when Hindu kings built fortified hilltop cities. A Muslim sultan conquered the prosperous valley three centuries later and introduced the faith that still binds the nation.

Though tiny and hard to reach, the northwest frontier is a cosmopolitan place, a centuries-old amalgam of invaders, migrants, traders, and refugees. A young Afghan refugee flashes a shy grin; when older, she'll wear a veil or a chador, a billowing robe covering all but her eyes. An Afghan man poses with his camel, the universal beast of burden along the frontier. He sports a pakhol, *the Tudor-like cap that is the traditional badge of Chitrali mountain men. A 72-year-old shopkeeper from the Kagan Valley, who caravanned through China and Afghanistan, wears the customary turban of Afghan men.*

The brown hair and eyes of a Kagan Valley girl bespeak her Indo-European ancestry. She'll probably never put on a veil, which would interfere with field work. Nor will this non-Muslim Kalash woman, who protects her fair skin with a paste of burned millet.

it must have been like when Genghis Khan and his hordes plundered their way across Central Asia more than 700 years ago.

Some of that surging Mongol blood now flows in Chitral, along with many other strains, some pure, others bewilderingly mixed. Here are people whose ancestors came from the most distant parts of China, others who arrived in caravans from the Indian plains. Every shade of skin color is here, even the palest, with red hair and blue eyes to match, in which case tradition says it is the result of couplings made with Macedonians when Alexander the Great passed through. Doubtless the latest turbulence along the frontier will leave other hereditary marks.

Just up the valley from Chitral Bazaar, an encampment of Afghan *mujahideen* and their families has been settled since soon after the Soviet invasion of their country, which is only a cock stride over the hill. Some are Tajiks from the Panjsher Valley, where stout resistance goes on; others are from Badakhshan, where the best polo ponies have traditionally been reared. Not all these refugees and fighters will go home again, even if the Russians do one day pull out. They will add another ingredient to the already astonishing variety of people in what is quite a small territory. Khowar is the chief language of Chitral, but so isolated and self-contained are some of its settlements that ten other local tongues are spoken as well.

The most remarkable of such people are the 2,500 or so Kalash, who speak Kalasha and inhabit three valleys in the south of Chitral, which were ignored by most outsiders until a road was introduced in 1976. Surrounded by Muslims, they have retained their ancient, animistic religion. Known nowhere else, it was once shared by other Kafirs ("infidels") who practiced it in nearby Kafiristan until the Emir of Afghanistan forcibly converted them to Islam in the 1890s. He thereupon renamed their homeland Nuristan—"land of light."

At the head of the Kalash pantheon is Dezao, the great creator, and lesser gods include

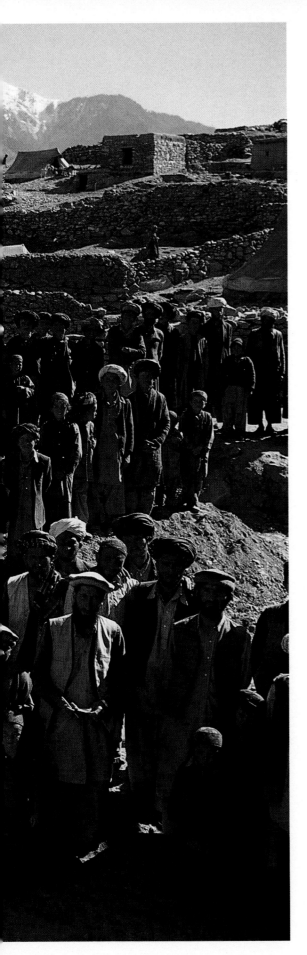

Pangs of homelessness and loneliness, of grief over slain parents and maimed children, unite Afghan refugees at a camp downriver from Chitral. Many mujahideen *slip back through the Hindu Kush to attack the Soviets, then return to this refuge. "We will fight to the last blood of a small child," proclaimed one defiant Afghan.*

Pakistanis welcomed their neighbors in the name of Muslim hospitality—"There are no gates, no fences, no barbed wire," said one official—but now must cope with the world's largest refugee population. Some fear that the newcomers will take away jobs and burden a sorely strained economy.

The Soviet invasion of Afghanistan adds another episode to the century-long contest between Russia and the West for control of the Indian subcontinent. Dubbed "the great game" during the British heyday, this struggle unifies the peoples of the northwest frontier.

Sajigor (deity of shepherds and their flocks), Jestak (the home and family), and Mahandeo (honeybees). They are worshiped with blood sacrifice of goats, and the Kalash villages are also notable for strange wooden carvings of human beings astride horses. This is puzzling, for no horse has been kept in the valleys of Brumboret, Birir, and Rumbur within folk memory, the ground being broken by many torrential streams and too treacherously steep and rough for such animals.

It is a lenient faith on the whole, and its women enjoy a degree of freedom that neighboring Muslims might find shocking if they knew much about it. Purdah is distinctly absent, though long black dresses are worn, and young women often perform in public a dance similar to the undulating, circling *hasapiko* of the Greeks—in which some people see a further connection with Alexander the Great. Every summer, each village in the Birir Valley chooses its *bodalak*, a young man who spends the next month or two living apart as a shepherd but is given the best food available. When the Porh festival is held in September, he comes down to the village and offers to serve any married woman who is still without child.

Such a primitive social relic could survive today only in one of the most secret byways of mankind, though how much longer it will remain is anybody's guess. The other valleys of the Kalash abandoned the ritual of the bodalak some years ago. Chitral as a whole is a strange survival, almost hidden away up there near the roof of the world. I myself came to it across the Lawarai Pass, in one of the first jeeps to get through after a particularly bitter winter. We slithered across sheets of ice, drove blindly through a snowstorm on top of the pass, then came down to the warmth and loveliness of spring on the other side. I was reminded of James Hilton's old classic *Lost Horizon*. And it seemed to me that I, too, had stumbled into a Shangri-La.

By Geoffrey Moorhouse
Photographs by George F. Mobley

184

Riders of the Celestial Mountains

When autumn comes to the mountains of China's far west, so do the snows. They come lightly at first, no more than a dusting. But then, as September advances, the snows build and they begin to push the Kazak and Kirgiz shepherds from the splendid isolation of their summer camps and into the valleys below.

Day by day they file out of the mountains, the men, women, and children on horseback. They whistle to keep their sheep moving and sing to keep each other amused. They ride easily along a giddy mountain trail, now galloping after an errant goat or pony, now trotting out to meet an acquaintance who happens across the caravan, now leading a string of camels with all the family's possessions lashed aboard. They live with the seasons, accommodating their lives to the cycles of nature as they seek water and grass, two essentials of their existence.

Formerly the masters of Central Asia, the Kazaks and Kirgiz once roamed freely between China and the shores of the Caspian Sea, some of them as allies of Genghis Khan. Now they live divided by the Sino-Soviet border, pressed on all sides by the modern age, their traditional movements restricted. They cannot cross the frontier, except by rare government permission.

About one million Kazaks and Kirgiz live inside the Chinese border. Most of these are in the Xinjiang Uygur Autonomous Region, a

Nomads travel through the silence of the Pamir Mountains on China's frontier with Russia.

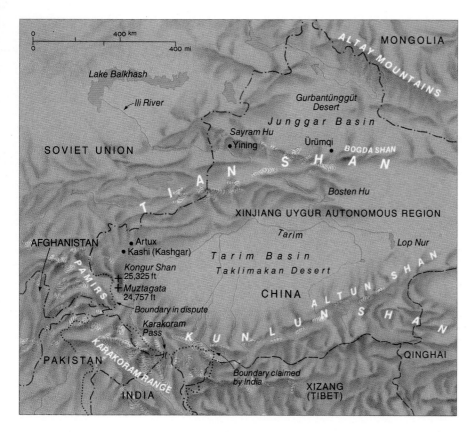

Young and still growing, the mountains—shan—of Xinjiang in China's far west push steadily skyward, a result of the Indian subcontinent grinding into the Eurasian landmass.

buffer about twice the size of Texas that separates China from its neighbors. Most Kazaks and Kirgiz never meet, even though they speak a similar language and share many customs. About 900,000 Kazaks live in northern Xinjiang—in the Tian Shan and Altay Mountains; Chinese Kirgiz, of whom there are some 110,000, live in the dry south—on the southern slopes of the Tian Shan and in the Pamir Mountains.

Xinjiang—"new dominion" in Chinese—is a frontier as forbidding physically as it is politically, bounded on one side by immense deserts and on three others by snow peaks of more than 20,000 feet. Given the inhospitable terrain, it is easy to understand why, until this century, the region was isolated, except from those travelers who crossed between Asia and Europe on the old Silk Road. But even those adventurers hurried across Xin-

jiang, fearful of the imaginary demons that were said to haunt the area and the very real bandits who did.

"Even by daylight," Marco Polo wrote of the region, "men hear the voices of Spirits, and often you fancy you are listening to the strains of many instruments, especially drums and the clash of arms. Travelers make a point of staying close together." No Great Wall was necessary to guard this part of Asia; natural boundaries were enough.

By the second week in September, most of the grass is gone from the place the Kazaks call Grassy Valley, deep in the Tian Shan—the Celestial Mountains. I arrived at the mouth of this valley late one afternoon to find a Kazak named Alwan Bay breaking camp.

Alwan Bay motioned me inside his yurt, the kind of conical felt tent that serves as home for most Kazaks, and began the conversation with an apology: "My hospitality is lacking," he said. "Under ordinary circumstances I would kill a lamb for you, and we would have a feast. But my relatives have already taken our herd around the mountain for the winter quarters. I am very sorry."

But the nomadic code of hospitality is strong—so strong that some Kazaks will pour milk in the dust for the snakes that slither by—and Alwan Bay insisted that his guest share what the family had on hand: bread, cheese, and a soothing goat-milk tea, served in bowls, which sent steam coiling up through the tent's open dome. Outside, the shadows lengthened toward the last night of Alwan Bay's summer.

"Summer in this place is good," he said, "but now the nights are cold, and we have to pile on more clothing. The grass is no longer rich. We will leave this place tomorrow."

As Alwan Bay talked, his wife and children made ready for tomorrow's journey, rolling up rugs and stacking firewood in the chill air. Two other families were taking down their own yurts just across the valley, finishing the task in half an hour. A woman named Gülazi supervised her family's last-minute packing. Her husband had departed Grassy Valley the day before, with one son and their 130 sheep. Gülazi would join him at their winter house, a stone hut two days away on horseback, and she was looking forward to the change.

"All the family will be together again, and the jobs will be easier," she said, eyeing her seven children who remained in camp. She found some carpets and spread them on the ground. We sat in the open air by a smoldering pine fire, drank our tea, and listened as one son, a skinny teenager with a cigarette, strummed a *dombera,* the two-stringed guitar that no Kazak family lacks.

The boy sang about travel, mountains, love, and horses—four constants in a Kazak's life—and he played beautifully. When he was done, night had closed like a lid over Grassy Valley. The darkness, along with the keen air and sudden silence, jolted everyone closer to the fire. The Tian Shan towered all around, steep and impenetrable. These mountains, so threatening to outsiders, sheltered Gülazi and her family, and down through the years, all the other people of her tribe. In their isolation, the nomads of Xinjiang developed as a people apart, one that could melt into the highlands when outsiders threatened, one that could withstand the occasional domination of China or Russia, but never for long.

Legally but not culturally a part of China, most nomads live under a measure of autonomy granted by the central government in Beijing. They follow their own relaxed form of Islam, have as many children as they please, keep their own animals for private profit, and wear their own hats as a badge of tribal honor. They even speak their own language, a rolling, musical tongue that came to Central Asia from Turkey in the sixth century—one reason Xinjiang was once known to the outside world as East Turkestan, or "land of the Turks." Most Kazaks and Kirgiz do not speak or understand Chinese, and many will look you square in the eye and say that they count themselves first as Kazak or Kirgiz and Chinese second or not at all.

The very name Kazak, which means "a free person, an adventurer," says something

Bruce Dale, National Geographic Photographer

about how they prefer to live. (The same name, altered by Slavic pronunciation, was adopted by the cavalrymen known as Russian Cossacks, unrelated, except perhaps in spirit, to the Kazaks of Central Asia.)

"We value our liberty," said Jinger Janabel, a Kazak student studying history at Xinjiang University in Ürümqi. "We want to manage for ourselves without being told how to behave." Over the years, that desire for independence has prompted the nomads to pick up and leave when more powerful nations threatened their way of life.

That is how Anayet, a Soviet-born Kazak, came to live in China. He and I met within a few miles of the Sino-Soviet border near Yining, where the land has the desolate beauty of the Scottish highlands—rolling mountains with granite outcrops.

From over one mountain, Anayet appeared

A Kazak boy peers from his family's tent, or yurt, near Ürümqi. China's nomads live on an uneasy frontier—a place noted for both its political and geological tumult. As the Himalayas rise, they block rainfall from the south; that, combined with Xinjiang's deep inland location, makes the region one of Earth's driest. In southern Xinjiang, most of the water comes from snowmelt, which flows from the mountains in warm weather.

Within the small world of a Kirgiz tent, a warming stove, a pot of milk tea, and the family circle . . . all offer respite from the rigors of a nomadic life. A strict protocol applies: Horsewhips are left outside; newlyweds get sleeping space behind the decorated reed screen; everyone avoids stepping on the dastorkon, *or tablecloth; guests sit facing the door on a carpet called* altegat, *six layers thick. All are expected, after dinner, to belch their appreciation and say a prayer of thanks to Allah.*

Pages 188-189: Sand dunes dwarf horses and riders in a Pamir meadow. Nearly constant winds buffet the sands of Xinjiang's Tarim Basin, creating huge dunes—so big they can be photographed by orbiting satellites.

Galen Rowell

like a visitation, galloping up alone, an old man in a cloud of dust. He dismounted his pony in a single, fluid motion. He was 64, and a life of hard work had kept him fit: ruddy, lean, and obviously proud, a Kazak at a glance. His trousers, threadbare at the seat and knees from long hours in the saddle, were tucked into tall leather riding boots. He wore a white felt hat and a wispy goatee, and there was something in his gaze that suggested he was not a fellow to be joshed with.

In the 1930s the Soviet government rounded up nomads throughout Central Asia and forced them to work on state farms. Anayet, then a boy of nine, was sent with his family to a place called Kalkous.

"We worked hard, but they gave us only enough food to stay alive," Anayet said. "Even the children worked. Finally my grandfather refused to work, and we left." The family of six fled on foot, at night, picking their way toward China, sleeping in caves when they were lucky enough to find them.

"We took no animals—just the clothes we were wearing and a small sack of wheat flour." The food was barely enough. "We were not only hungry, we were afraid that the Russian police would catch us."

But the police never did. After nine days Anayet's family arrived in China. His grandparents, worn by the journey, died almost immediately. For some 20 years after that, he was free to live the nomadic life once more. Then China had its own Communist revolution, and he found himself behind a plow again, this time on a collective in Xinjiang.

"It was bad here," he said with a nervous laugh and a glance at the party officials who attended our interview, "but better than in the Soviet Union. At least we had food to eat." He was reluctant to say more, given the audience, but I later learned that his story ended happily. He is a nomad once more, thanks to China's new economic reforms, which allow citizens to engage in some free enterprise. Anayet owns more than a hundred sheep, ten horses, fifteen cows, several yurts. In this mountain world he is a rich man.

Designed for mobility, the yurt has served the nomads of Central Asia for hundreds of years. A Kazak family breaks camp in China's Celestial Mountains, removing the felt flaps that form the tent's sides. Strong enough to stand against 90-mile-an-hour winds, the tent is buttressed by poplar poles; they fit into a circular top-piece called the xangerak. *A Kazak youth helps by readying a* xangerak *for packing. Yurts can be erected or taken down in an hour, but the word for this temporary shelter literally means "home."*

Kazaks secure their cargo on a two-humped Bactrian camel, which provides milk and can carry half-ton loads.

"I prefer the traveling life to farming," he said, raising one big hand toward the blue autumn sky. And his feeling toward his Soviet birthplace? He frowned and spoke quietly, almost in a whisper: "I dislike even looking at that side of the mountains."

The traveling life that seems so dear to Anayet is a hard one, filled with discomfort and the occasional danger brought on by the whims of nature. A late snow during the spring migration—when the ewes are pregnant and the flock is still weak from winter—can destroy a family's wealth in a single stroke. And there is the insistent cold that finds you every night. And the dryness that cracks your skin and makes it bleed. And the grime and dust that accumulate, day after day, on people and clothing because water is so scarce it cannot be wasted on baths. And the diet, always the same: milk and mutton, bread and milk, mutton and milk. Finally, there is the isolation that limits medical care and surely contributes to the staggering rate of stillbirths in Xinjiang's mountains.

Despite all that, many nomads prefer their way, tenuous as it may be, to the settled life of a farmer or factory worker. "As long as we have mutton to eat and milk to drink, it is good for us," says one, echoing a sentiment I heard all over the mountains. In the past, in fact, wealthy Kazaks hired servants to stay at home so that they themselves were free to live in tents, ride through the mountains, and graze their flocks—a reversal of the pattern familiar in the American West, where monied ranchers stayed at home as soon as they could afford it, hiring riders to tend the herd.

If you fly over the Tian Shan, you can see why it took centuries for the government to subdue these highlanders: Until the age of the airplane, the mountains were inviolate; no government could easily pursue and find the people who fled there. The snow peaks swirl with clouds, and in between, the rumpled ridges pile one upon the other in a maze, overlapping and compressing in fantastic convolutions, like the folds of a human brain.

Now and again a high thin valley appears through the clouds, a faint line of green crisscrossed by silver streams, and in each valley a khaki dot or two—Kazak yurts. The yurts rarely cluster in anything approaching the dimensions of a village, but lie sprinkled about the mountains, one family here, one over there, each keeping its distance from the other so that all will have adequate grazing.

One wonders how such a scattered tribe could keep their identity, especially in the face of the frequent turmoil that has beset them. Perhaps these people, like the Scots or Jews, take strength from past or present threats—threats that make their precarious culture more precious still, a thing to be nourished by family and clan.

"The turmoil only makes us more stubborn to keep our own nation united," said Abdul Kadir, a Kirgiz scholar living in Artux. "We cannot survive if we do not maintain our own style and our own customs."

Kirgiz and Kazak also rely on a strong oral tradition, which helps to keep their people cohesive. By this network, information moves back and forth across the mountains. Ordinary travelers are expected to relay the latest news about neighbors from the next valley. And when there is a wedding or funeral, friends gather from miles around to recite poetry and to sing epic songs. There may also be races and games celebrating the horse, still the prime transportation in these mountains.

"Horses are the wings of our people," says an old Kirgiz proverb. As if in gratitude, nomads lavish attention on a favorite horse, outfitting it with a brilliantly colored saddle. In Kazak regions a *juwax at,* or honest horse, holds an honored position; so it is still considered a serious personal insult to the owner if you criticize his horse. By the same token, it is polite to compliment a bride by saying she looks like a horse.

But nothing outranks the importance of family in the world of Kazak and Kirgiz. They depend upon each other for work, and they live together for months on end without seeing outsiders. I routinely asked each of my hosts the same question: "Of the following

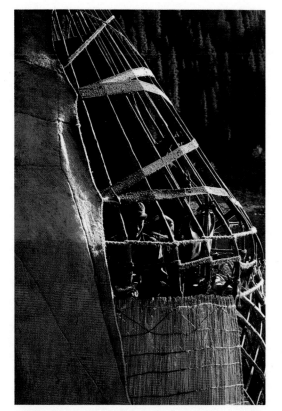

Galen Rowell

The turbulent history of a restless people etches the face of a Kirgiz herdsman. His ancestors, pressed by invading armies and settlers, fled their Mongolian homeland in the tenth century and began to wander Central Asia. Like Kazaks, a related people, Kirgiz display a range of racial features, combining their Mongolian and Turkish ancestry.

Robert M. Poole, National Geographic Staff (also above and center)

things, which is most important to you—motherland, livestock, freedom, security, God, or family?" Family always came first.

Parents keep family histories in their heads, passing along the information to their children. I met a Kazak in his 80s who could tick off, one by one, the names of his ancestors to 18 generations—some 1,200 years back. When a Kazak named Turde Ahun told me he had seven children, I asked if they were enough: "Not really," he said. "We would like to have more if Allah would assist us." More children mean a prosperous life, more hands for keeping more livestock.

Toward the end of day, Turde Ahun's family starts gathering in a valley campsite northeast of Yining, where they will spend one of the last nights of their autumn migration. A brother holds a horse as Turde Ahun trims its hoof for a new shoe. A son and daughter ride in from opposite directions, herding sheep. As a half-moon rises above the Tian Shan, son and daughter begin to count the sheep, to make sure all 230 are present. They are. To protect them, the whole family will go without sleep tonight, patrolling the camp's perimeter to watch for wolves.

Turde Ahun's neighbor piles camel dung and pine branches on the fire, which smolders and pops under a caldron. The smell of boiling lamb drifts on the wind, while Turde Ahun blitzes me with questions. "How much money do you make?" he wants to know. "Do you drive a car? Could I use one here? When you cannot understand our language, do you get lonely? Do all Americans kiss in public?"

This last question, to which I answered no, was prompted by an American movie Turde Ahun saw last year, at a community center near his winter quarters. Like others of his tribe, he is curious about the outside world. He keeps track of it, most of the time, with a battery-powered radio. He has two of those, but his proudest possession, he shows me, is a portable tape player.

Next morning, before Turde Ahun's family moves down the valley, the tape machine is the last thing to be packed on the camel's

In the fleeting summer of the Celestial Mountains, Kazak riders watch over their herd. Here melting snows feed lush pastures, which, in turn, produce a breed of horses known for its swiftness, strength, and stamina. From the second century B.C., *Chinese emperors sought these horses for their armies; the monarchs traded precious tea to get the famous steeds they called the Heavenly Stallions.*

Xinjiang yields to new development as Chinese settlers migrate to exploit mineral wealth and carve huge farms from the grasslands. Since Communist control came in 1949, more than a hundred state farms have been established, and land under cultivation has doubled.
Galen Rowell

back. It rides on top like a prize.

Frost glitters on the yellow grass as we point our ponies away from the morning sun. We ride down through October meadows, surrounded by spruces and jagged snow peaks that give this land the look of Montana. The cold air fairly crackles, so pure and thin that a magpie's chirp resonates for what seems like a mile. The trail drops toward the immense blue lake called Sayram, where our caravan arrives by early afternoon; the ponies wade in and drink their fill, slurping and tossing their heads. Along the graveled shore a falcon hunts, its quick shadow flicking across the land.

The last stage of Turde Ahun's journey will take the caravan northward. Animals and riders take to the new blacktop road, where there is the shock of diesel fumes, rumbling buses, and blaring horns. After days of solitude, the highway intrudes on the senses, as much for pony as for rider. The ponies spook, and it is all I can do to hold mine, even when I get off and walk him. He rolls his eyes and lunges toward the mountains. Turde Ahun, who has a stronger hand, rides calmly ahead, intent on getting to his winter home.

Bit by bit, the grasslands of Xinjiang are dwindling, given over to new coal mines and oil fields, to timber operations and high-rise cities, to sprawling farms run by Chinese colonists from the heartland, who have swollen Xinjiang's population by almost five million since the 1950s. New highways are planned, and local government officials speak glowingly of Xinjiang as China's California, a land of hope, promise, and profit. By the year 2000, a ranking government official in Ürümqi tells me, the herdsmen like Turde Ahun will roam no more. "They will live in one place with their animals, not scattered around as they are now."

So that is the plan for Turde Ahun, whose kin survived conquest after conquest. Can they survive the future?

By Robert M. Poole
Photographs by Thomas Nebbia

Bruce Dale, National Geographic Photographer

Robert M. Poole, National Geographic Staff (also right, center)

As in Marco Polo's day, the bazaar of Kashi (Kashgar) still buzzes with commerce. Uygurs buy and sell the bright dresses favored by Muslim women, even those of the conservative Sunni sect, here veiled in brown. Fiery peppers, fresh vegetables, and a specialty called mare's teat grapes add zest to the local diet. Agriculture prospers in these deserts because of irrigation and aqueducts that bring precious water from the mountains to cities like Kashi and Ürümqi.

Traditionally, Turkic-speaking Uygurs and other Muslims have outnumbered all other groups and dominated life in Xinjiang, but Chinese settlers are changing that. Han farmers, like this wheat thresher near Ürümqi (opposite), comprise some 40 percent of Xinjiang's population—up from just 6 percent in 1953.

A Lesotho village nestles on a peak overlooking South Africa.

Nicholas DeVore III

WORLDS APART

The highest peaks within South Africa lie in the tiny enclave Kingdom of Lesotho. Culturally distinct from surrounding lowlanders, Lesotho's people struggled to gain recognition as a separate nation only two decades ago. Now they find themselves economically dependent upon South Africa.

Isolated by geography and sometimes by choice, highlanders everywhere tend to be aloof, self-reliant, and conservative—traits that nowadays may yield to the realities of economic need and political relationships. Few now are the isolated worlds that 19th-century geographer Ellen Semple called "museums of social antiquities."

But shepherds from New Zealand's Southern Alps to Spain's Pyrenees live miles from their neighbors. Berbers in the High Atlas of Morocco speak a different dialect from other Berbers. Highland tribes in Papua New Guinea only recently encountered the 20th century.

Home of the Basques

A"*rrotz erri, otso erri*—The land of strangers is a land of wolves." Among the sheepherding mountain Basques of Spain and France, the wolf is the primordial enemy, the predator against which the shepherd has protected his flock with special fury. Today wolves are almost gone from these mountains. What has not changed is the desire of this ancient and mysterious people to remain independent and isolated. For Basques still divide their world into strangers and friends, predators and prey, wolves and sheep.

I am an outsider, but the mountain Basques have never treated me like one. My wife is Basque, and the heritage runs through the veins of our three children. We have often visited Euskadi, as the Basques call their homeland. On the train ride north from Madrid, we always know when we enter Basque country. The landscape changes—from the brown, arid plateau of Castile to the green, moist mountains of Euskadi. I remember our first car trip through narrow mountain passes on the road from Pamplona to Guipúzcoa Province. I had returned from Vietnam only a few years before, and I thought, strangely, how much the Basque mountains resembled Vietnam's central highlands. The similarity, I learned later, goes beyond the roughness of the terrain; the Basque mountains, like those of Vietnam, gave sanctuary to a small army of insurgents.

Backs straight, feet flying, Basque dancers step into their ancient art.

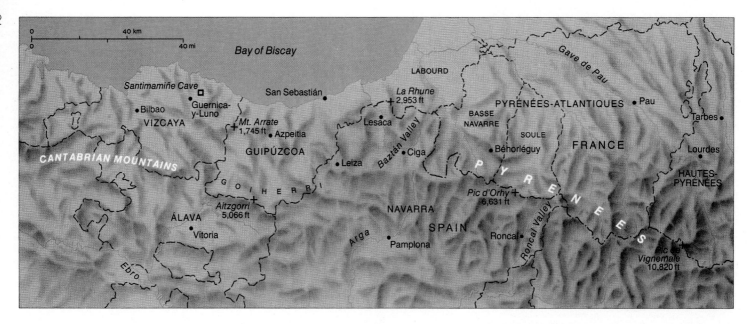

The Pyrenees have built a 270-mile rampart from the Mediterranean to the Bay of Biscay—mostly gentle and wooded to the west, where they meet the Cantabrian Mountains. Seven provinces of Spain and France, an area about the size of New Jersey, make the Basque homeland. Mountain seclusion has been one safeguard of the Basque culture; another is the conservative, clannish nature of these people whose ancient origin is unknown.

Christmas Eve of 1978 found us in the small town of Leiza, where—like American youngsters anticipating Santa Claus—Basque children awaited the red-eyed, sooty-faced *olentzero,* a mythical charcoal burner who descends from the wooded mountain slopes to the village on the night before Christmas. The olentzero leaves presents for the good girls and boys, and lumps of charcoal for the bad ones.

As the Pyrenees begin their descent toward the Bay of Biscay and the point where the Iberian coast turns north into France, they meet a second mountain chain, the Cantabrians. This is the heart of the Basque mountain country. Throughout the mountains and valleys radiating from this intersection are signs that people have lived here for millennia. From the Baztán Valley in northern Navarra to Santimamiñe near Guernica are prehistoric cave paintings of deer, horses, bears, and bison. The remains of Stone Age chambered tombs known as dolmens abound throughout the region.

In southern Guipúzcoa the overgrown cobblestones of San Adrian's Road remind us that the Romans were here near the beginning of the Christian era. Ceremonies born in the Middle Ages persist. One is the Tribute of the Three Cows, a ritual observed every summer since 1375 in the pass above the Roncal Valley, where the mayors of the French Basque villages deliver livestock to village mayors of the Spanish side, in exchange for grazing rights. For centuries these green hills and valleys shielded the Basque culture and language. Today there are roads, commerce and tourism, radio and television. The Basques no longer enjoy independence from the wolves of the modern world.

On our most recent visit we drove along a narrow, winding road to the top of Mount Arrate, a misty peak on the border between Guipúzcoa and Vizcaya. The July afternoon was gray and chilly as it is almost year-round on the Cantabrian coast. We were on our way to meet my wife's two sisters and their families—more than forty of us in all—for a reunion. We planned a family lunch with their 75-year-old uncle, parish priest of Our Lady of Arrate, the stone church and sanctuary at the top of the mountain. Before Tío Pedro joined us, he officiated at a wedding and, before we knew it, we were drawn into the par-

ty. What we saw that afternoon—the blend of old and new—repeated itself again and again throughout the summer.

The church building has stood on the mountaintop since 1498, six years after Columbus first sailed to the New World. From the ceiling hung a model of a fishing ship, the emblem of special prayers for the Basque fishermen who have followed their trade since prehistoric times. Music for the afternoon came from instruments that have been traditional among Basques for hundreds of years—the flutelike *txistu,* with its high piercing notes, and the *tamboril,* a small drum beaten with a single drumstick. Young *dantzariak* performed dances that originated in the Middle Ages or earlier—perhaps even before Christianity. They did the energetic sword dance, with running leaps and raised blades; then the graceful, ceremonial *aurresku,* often danced in honor of visiting dignitaries, where an intricate chain of men and women step in and out to a formal air.

The groom was Basque, the bride Spanish, and Tío Pedro conducted the ceremony in both Spanish and Euskara, or Basque, a language that has been called the oldest in the

world. A young woman in the wedding party recorded the ceremony on videotape, using a camera manufactured in Japan. Probably it will be seen over and over on television sets made in Germany or the Netherlands.

Until the middle of this century, many mountain Basques spent their lives in a world no more than ten or twenty miles from the house where they were born. In the old days, such seclusion gave rise to mythical characters like the olentzero, who is a variation of the *basajaun,* or man of the woods. The basajaun is a huge, ferocious, bearded creature of remote mountain forests, rarely seen by villagers or shepherds.

A real life basajaun was the charcoal maker, whose solitary, dangerous life made him an object of awe. Once there were hundreds of charcoal makers. Now their superhuman strength and courage, and their proud independence of the entanglements of modern life live on in legends.

The people who live in these mountains know that their roots reach deep, but most seem to take this heritage for granted. In Leiza the son of the Zabaleta family, Patxi, told us that the *(Continued on page 208)*

"Before God was God and boulders were boulders, the Basques were already Basques." So say descendants of the mysterious people who have lived in the western Pyrenees for at least 5,000 years. The Basque farmers gathered here to discuss a livestock sale belong to a population distinguished by blood type, physical features, ancient customs, and a fierce independence. Some 700,000 Basques speak their unique language, called the oldest in the world.

Pages 204-205: The fields of this French Basque farm are typically lush, green—and steep. Often, farmers cultivate and harvest with animals and hand tools.

Pages 206-207: In tourist-packed Pamplona, Spain, the July Feast of San Fermín brings to the streets fiesta-garbed men and fighting bulls running for the arena. Rolled newspapers are sometimes tools of machismo for those who outrun the bull just slowly enough to hit it on the nose.

family home is the "new house," a weather-beaten, stone *baserria* built in 1542. It replaces a house on the same site that had been burned in one of the frequent border wars of that era between Navarrese and Guipúzcoans. Another Basque farmer, near Leiza, Miguel Sagaztibeltza, admitted proudly that his family had lived in his baserria for 325 years, but his amused reaction to my question told me that this was not something he thought much about until outsiders brought up the subject.

West of the Pyrenees-Cantabrian junction is a region known as the Goiherri, from the Basque for "highlands." The Goiherri is a focus of Basque culture and the center of the insurgency for independence from Spain—another element in Basque life that has deep roots. In these valleys Euskara hangs on tenaciously; as many as 80 percent of the people speak it. In Leiza almost all the 3,000 citizens are bilingual. When we attended Mass in Leiza, the priest read the Gospel in flowing Spanish, but to reach the people, in his sermon he switched to the more direct Euskara.

Whether because the Catholic Church is strong in Basque life or because isolated mountain people anywhere tend to cling to tradition, the Goiherri is a conservative region. Logically, conservative politics should dominate, yet Basque nationalist parties of the left and center win most elections. Shortly after our visit, Spanish Guardia Civil troops battled in the streets with youths seeking to hang a Basque nationalist flag from the town hall balcony.

Leading the insurgency is an underground organization known as ETA, an acronym for Euskadi ta Askatasuna, or Basque Homeland and Liberty. For generations the mountains have sheltered fighters for independence. Since the 1960s the Goiherri has been the prime source for ETA recruits and a focus of attacks against the hated Guardia Civil.

Not all the Basque mountain towns are experiencing the turmoil of change. In Ciga, a village off the main road midway up the

A Spanish festival in the land of the Basques, San Fermín honors the seventh-century bishop of Pamplona. Fermín, martyred when dragged by a bull, became the patron saint of bullfighters. Parades, costumes, street bands, and much wine from the porrón enliven the week-long fiesta. Children taunt a cabezudo (left, lower), who will solemnly and harmlessly thwack them on the head. A victorious matador circles Pamplona's bullring (opposite) in the culmination of the Spanish ritual entertainment.

Tourism and modern industrialism dilute the close-knit Basque culture, bringing ever more outside influences even to mountain Basques. San Fermín means the opportunity for political demonstration to a peña, a social club (left, upper) whose banner protests Spanish entry into NATO.

Baztán Valley, we saw at least a dozen old ba-serriak. Near the church of San Lorenzo, flower boxes bear carved figures representing Ciga's principal occupations: carpentry, stock raising and butchering, farming and vine culture. Despite the television antennas that sprout from baserriak, and reception in Spanish, French, and Basque, not much has changed in Ciga. The town remains what it has always been—a cluster of baserriak, each with its lands and livestock. Generally, however, such places are being left behind.

It had been 15 years since my first visit to the Basque mountains. Almost everywhere I saw signs of change. Tourists from Spain, France, and beyond invade at an increasing rate. Their presence will bring to an end some of the old ways. High up in the mountains, there is a kind of baserria that the shepherd uses while he is with the sheep in the high summer pastures. These remote, rustic buildings may be little more than stone huts for protection from the weather. In earlier times, shepherds left them unlocked. Nowadays, weekend hunters from the cities rent—or simply appropriate—vacant huts. When they depart, they leave behind the debris of modernity, the cans and bottles that now litter the mountainsides.

Tourist influence overshadows the saints' festivals celebrated from spring to fall in nearly every Basque town—San Ignacio in Azpeitia, San Fernando in Leiza, San Fermín in Pamplona. Youths still dance the Basque jota to the lively accordion into the early morning; muscular farm boys still try their hand at weight lifting, log chopping, testing teams of oxen. But often there are spectacles from outside: traveling carnivals with Ferris wheels and bumper cars; street vendors selling cheap plastic goods from Hong Kong; rock bands blaring away in the plaza.

The still rich timber stands and a reliable labor force have attracted light industry to the mountains. In 1957 a paper mill opened in Leiza. At its height it employed some 1,500 workers and spurred a population boom. Apartment buildings for the new workers

The view eastward from the Roncal Valley, on the edge of Basque country, looks toward the higher central Pyrenees. Pleistocene glaciers scraped the U-shaped valleys. Even on the less rugged slopes to the west, farming is not easy. Women near Lesaca, Spain, deliver milk from their mountain farm to the collection point on the main road. Near Béhorléguy, France, a Basque farmer carries hay for winter storage. Basque tradition holds that the most honorable life is one of self-sufficiency and hard work on the land.

Pages 212-213: As immutable as its stone walls, the baserria has been the foundation of Basque society. These farmsteads are passed on, generation after generation, to a single family heir.

A Basque girl stands in her home, in the midst of preparations to celebrate her first Communion. The most lavish feast a family can afford is traditional on ritual occasions. Basques are devout Roman Catholics, although until the Middle Ages they were held to be pagan. The church is a strong, unifying force in Basque social life and in the Basque movement for political separation from Spain and France.

sprang up alongside 300-year-old baserriak. Now the Basque country shares the economic decline felt by all of Spain, and the paper mill has cut its work force in half. Leiza's population is back at its normal level. To tell the truth, many residents do not seem upset at this turn. They recognize that despite the prosperity, the paper mill jeopardized traditional values. Today the older townspeople complain about the young people who are leaving the baserriak for the *fiestas sin fin,* or endless parties, of the big cities.

The baserria is more than a building and a way of exploiting the land. It is also a family identity. The home of the Zabaleta family in Leiza is a typical *kaleko* baserria, inside the town limits. Señor Zabaleta grows a vegetable garden and keeps only a cow or two. The produce supplements the chief source of income, usually from a job with a local factory or other firm. Señor Zabaleta worked, until his retirement, as a night watchman in the paper mill.

In the mountains outside Leiza, the three-century-old Sagaztibeltza home is a *mendiko* baserria. The family consists of Miguel, in his 30s, and his mother and father. The farm was built by Señor Sagaztibeltza's ancestors upon their return from the American colonies, where they had accumulated a small stake. Most baserriak have names, and the name of this one—Indiana Borda, or Indian Farm— reflects its origin in the New World. On this baserria, the family depends entirely on the farm. Crops feed people and animals. For cash, Miguel sells milk to a local dairy cooperative. Spain's entry into the European Common Market has meant that Miguel must invest in equipment and renovation to meet competition from dairy producers of other nations. To him, as a proud Basque, this is a loss of independence.

Like most baserriak, Indiana Borda is a massive, three-story structure of huge stones covered with whitewashed plaster. The roof, supported by thick oak beams cut from the surrounding forests, was originally made of heavy slabs of slate. Now it is the more com-

When Basques reenact traditional festivities, they dance. Here, at an old-style wedding, merrymakers revive the traditional jota (opposite). As part of the procession, a young woman carries a brass vessel, and a man leads an ox. Traditionally the oxcart bore the marriage bed, the hope chest, and other dowry items from the bride's old home to her new one. By custom, it is said, the ox pulled a cart with un-greased wheels. The squealing of the wheels made it seem that the bride's family had loaded the cart to the breaking point.

mon red tile. The ground floor of the baserria is given over to the stalls and pens that house cattle and pigs all year, and sheep during the winter when they cannot stay in the mountains. The rising body heat of the animals helps warm the upper floors during the cold, wet mountain winters. The third floor is the storage place for the hay that feeds the animals in the winter. From there a chute leads to the stable.

The second floor contains the family living quarters and the focus of the house—the kitchen. Over the main entrance hangs a hand-lettered plaque: *"Jaungoikoak Onetsi Bediz Etxe Onetako Bazter Guziak*—May God Bless Each Corner of This House." Furnishings throughout are spare and simple, but in the wide central hall stand four large chests, ornately hand carved and almost as old as the house.

Life in the baserria is hard and precarious. Miguel and his father do nearly all the work by hand or with light tractors, since the terrain does not lend itself to heavy machinery and there is little capital for mechanization anyway. Miguel's mother too does her chores by hand, cooking on a wood stove that is fueled by wood cut and carried by the family.

Today survival depends as much on prices in distant markets as it does on the health of the sheep in Miguel's flock or the amount of Cantabrian rainfall. Small wonder that many observers predict the demise of the baserria by the end of this century. Every year since 1975 there have been 4,000 fewer farming people in the Spanish Basque country. The young people are leaving. Miguel belongs to the small part—8 percent—of the Basque farm population under 40 years old. The average farmer is in his 50s. The picture is similar in the French provinces. Gloomy forecasts, however, fail to reckon with people like Miguel Sagaztibeltza. His family has lived in Indiana Borda for more than three centuries. He will not give it up now.

By Robert P. Clark
Photographs by William Albert Allard

Western Highlands women of Papua New Guinea beat out a ceremonial dance rhythm.

David Robert Austen

Patterns of Old & New

"**W**as it the sound of flood waters, or of an earthquake?" wondered Papua New Guinea's highlanders as the airplane roared closer. Then they saw it looming like a monstrous silver bird. "In terror they fell to the ground . . . ," wrote anthropologist Ronald M. Berndt, "not daring to look up again for fear they would be instantly killed. Rising at last, they melted some pigs' fat over a fire, and poured it upon the earth as a libation to the ancestral spirits."

Thus, in 1933, did tribes still living in the Stone Age greet the 20th century. The cloud-girt ranges of central Papua New Guinea, with many peaks topping 10,000 feet, had hidden until then the upland ridges and valleys where they lived. Tangled rain forests and treacherous swamps barred access from coastal lowlands.

Missionaries and gold prospectors had begun to penetrate the mountains in the 1920s, risking malaria and attacks from bands of cannibals. Then prospectors, flying over unexplored territory in 1933, spied a fertile valley 5,500 feet up, strewn with thatched houses and neat garden plots.

There and in the surrounding highlands, clans battled to survive in a world they believed to be ruled by capricious ancestral spirits. The men appeased them by offering them pig meat. Warriors fought over land, women, the illness or death of a relative

220 (an undoubted victim of sorcery), and pigs.

The women reared the pigs, sometimes suckling piglets alongside their children, and tended gardens of vegetables and sweet potatoes, the staple food. The tribes used pigs as currency—to pay for a bride, for instance, or to compensate an injury. A large number of wives, children, and pigs enhanced a man's prestige and he might become a local leader—called *bik man* in island pidgin. But his wealth and status depended mostly on how many repayment obligations he imposed by giving away pigs and other goods at pig exchanges or feasts.

Half a century has brought towns, highways, and the country's most important cash crop —coffee—to the highland provinces. About 80 percent of the nation's coffee is grown there, with mountain tribes producing an increasing proportion; it has

New Guinea lies on the southwestern curve of the Ring of Fire—the volcanic zone circling the Pacific. Tectonic activity left a legacy of minerals across the island. In the eastern half, now the nation of Papua New Guinea, the lure of gold led prospectors to the discovery of a dense tribal population living in valleys among the knifelike ridges of the central mountains. Their Stone Age world made headlines in the 1930s as the "last unknown."

David Gillison

edged their vegetable gardens onto poorer land. But many of their customs have not changed much, although they may serve new purposes.

Tribes living near provincial headquarters such as Mount Hagen or Goroka now entertain tourists with their *singsing* dances before a pig feast. Plastic beads and paint from the store often supplement the traditional body decorations of shells, feathers, and natural pigments. And a warrior may be happy to sell his ceremonial ax.

In remote Eastern Highlands villages, costumed performers traditionally act out tribal myths. Modern health authorities make good use of this theatrical custom: Masked actors in the guise of dogs, pigs, and flies dramatize the diseases that result from bad sanitation.

And tribes have made adaptations in ritual. Belief in the power of ancestral spirits may now blend with the magic brought by missionaries. In the sacred area that Simbu Province highlanders cleared for a pig kill, they raised a crucifix and asked the Catholic priest's blessing. The men piled an offering of pig fat around the crucifix.

Mary B. Dickinson

Husband and wife live separately in an Eastern Highlands compound, one of fifteen forming a village. The two round houses serve as dormitories for men and boys. Women share smaller dwellings with young children and sometimes pigs. Cooking fires warm inhabitants; the stifling smoke helps keep the thatch dry and thus water resistant. Signs of the times are foreign poinsettias and cash crops of coffee shaded by feathery casuarina trees.

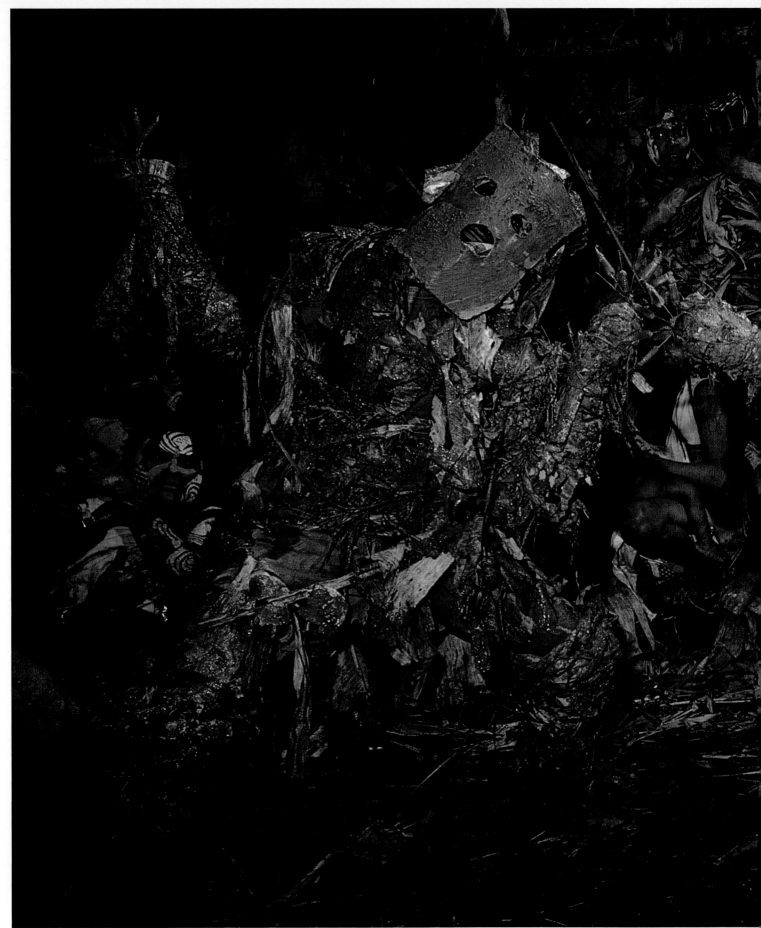

Clay-daubed villagers portray terrifying ancestral spirits from a tribal myth.

223

David Gillison

224

Danny Lehman

David Robert Austen, Stock Boston

Danny Lehman

Pig kills (far left), feasts, and competitive pig-meat exchanges channel energies once used in clan warfare, now officially banned. Highlanders initiate their sons into manhood and marry off their daughters at such potlatch-style festivals. Guests troop in (left) from surrounding villages, then hosts and guests dance and sing—a singsing in island pidgin.

Both sexes paint their bodies and create elaborate headdresses and chest pieces from feathers, marsupial furs, and shells. Men prize especially the plumes of male birds of paradise, symbols of masculine prowess. They may also wear a nose ornament or a leafy bustle called an asgras. From festival finery to a girl's facial tattoo, body decoration is the main visual art form of the highlands.

The pigs, ritually slaughtered, are cut up, layered with banana leaves in pits, and steamed. Hosts distribute pig meat to guests, earning honor and the expectation of repayment in kind at a return feast.

The World of the Mountain Berber

If any place in the High Atlas mountains has *baraka*—that sacred power bestowed by God—Jebel Azourki does. Local lore says that a cave near the mountain's 12,106-foot summit was destined to be the tomb of the Prophet Muhammad. But when the camel bearing his body arrived from Arabia, it was frightened by the noises the Aït Bou Guemmez Valley people make to shoo birds from their fields. The camel turned back to distant Mecca, and so must Moroccan pilgrims journey there, when they might only have had to climb Azourki.

Legends that invoke the Prophet to explain animist practices like mountain worship abound in Morocco's highlands. This is the domain of the Berbers (*imazighen*—free men, they call themselves), a tribal people who have inhabited Morocco for 2,000 years or more. In the seventh century the Arabs began their conquest of North Africa, and Islam soon took root, but in much of Berber Morocco ancient beliefs persist—in spirits, charms, holy mountains and trees, and the cult of local saints—often in an Islamic guise.

To reach the Aït Bou Guemmez Valley in summer takes four or five hours by car up a dirt road from Azilal, the nearest major town. The French built the road in the 1930s, after conquering the valley. Though they had ruled Morocco since 1912, it took some years

Patterned stonework fortifies a Berber home in the valley of the Aït Bou Guemmez.

With peaks over 12,000 feet, the High Atlas range separates the Sahara from Morocco's fertile lowlands and forms part of a mountain system extending 1,200 miles through Morocco, Algeria, and Tunisia.

mountain road had skirted the lush floor, bouncing and jostling me through a dozen similar settlements strung out every quarter mile or so. In the shade of an enormous walnut tree, Aisha waited her turn at the village well. Tattoos covered her forehead and chin; heavily hennaed sidelocks held by barrettes protruded from her headdress. As she explained why baraka infuses the Aït Bou Guemmez, a henna red hand gestured toward fields where, now in midsummer, potatoes, corn, and alfalfa ripened.

How had people come to settle in this remote place? I asked. They came "before the Portuguese," she said, "drawn by the many springs." To Aisha, as to many of her fellow tribespeople, these 15th-century invaders signal an eon long past, as far back as they know. No one knows how long the Bou Guemmez (Aït means "people of") have lived here or much else about their history.

Aisha's village, like most of the valley's 27 other villages, consists of a score of two- and three-story rectangular dwellings without electricity or running water. Behind it, and rimming the valley, are the foothills and peaks of the M'goun ridgeline, the country's longest single stretch of land above 12,000 feet. But this village is different; its inhabitants are *shurfa*, possessors of a holy lineage. Their ancestor, tradition says, was a 14th-century saint from across Jebel Azourki who descended from the Prophet. His baraka gives his male heirs a tendency toward sainthood, attainable in their lifetimes if they show certain personal qualities and powers.

"Come home with me," urged Aisha. "You will be welcome in my guest room." A group of her women friends were just then arriving to visit from other villages, their donkeys and mules kicking up clouds of dust. Hennaed sidelocks also framed their faces, the style for married women of the Bou Guemmez tribe. "Chief of the sweet-scented flowers of this world and of the next," the Prophet had called the henna plant, and so baraka permeates it. Women use its dye as a cosmetic and as protection from *jnun*—spirits, Aisha said.

to subdue the various Berber tribes who inhabited the Atlas. Known as the *bilad al siba*—land of dissidence—these highland regions had for centuries been controlled by powerful and warring chieftains, and were isolated from the rest of Morocco, the *bilad al makhzan*—land of the central government.

Strewn with rocks, the road to the Aït Bou Guemmez clings to the steep hillsides. It winds up and over the monotonous brown mounds of the High Atlas, one of four mountain ranges separating the coastal lowlands from the Sahara. Eventually, in the distance, an emerald patch emerges through the folds. As the road winds down, the patch gradually broadens into a narrow valley nearly 20 miles long, a highland oasis at 6,000 feet.

"We have water—the source of life," said a young widow named Aisha in Talsinant, a compact village deep in the valley. The

A stone-and-mud brick village grows out of a hillside in the Aït Bou Guemmez Valley, an oasis more than a mile high. A Berber tribe, the Bou Guemmez, inhabits this remote High Atlas area, isolated from mainstream Morocco. In these mountains millennia ago, the Berbers' ancestors found refuge from the Romans, who called them barbari—*barbarians.*

When the Arabs invaded in the seventh century, the mountain fastnesses helped guard Berber ethnic and linguistic identity. Today highland Berbers still speak their unwritten tongue and practice a religion that combines Islam with local beliefs and customs.

We dodged cows, goats, and chickens in the inner courtyard to follow Aisha up a dank staircase of crudely packed mud. Three doors opened off the landing; two of them led into bare rooms with adobe walls. Aisha's ancient, blind grandmother crouched in a dark corner, rocking and murmuring incantations in a Berber dialect of the High Atlas.

Then a surprise: The third room was finished, its walls whitewashed and its floor covered in thick wool rugs. Bright sunlight poured in through square, green-rimmed windows. An elaborate geometric pattern, painted black and yellow and turquoise, decorated the ceiling. A low table of tooled metal held a tea set, a cone of sugar, and a large bunch of mint. It was the guest room.

"We have no time to make such things to sell," said Aisha, when I inquired whether the rugs and women's spangled wool shawls were available at the weekly souk. "Our life is very hard; we seldom stop working. Only now that the barley harvest is over have we time to visit. Normally we work much harder than the men do." Aisha's half-dozen friends nodded and laughed, apparently unfazed by this inequity. "But life is good here. We have pure air and water and good food. And what work we do is all for us."

One guest named Fatima vehemently agreed. Dressed like the others in an ankle-length nylon gown and plastic slip-ons, she was home for a vacation from Casablanca, where her husband is a soldier. "It is healthier here for my children. In Casa I only keep house, but we have to pay for everything. Here I also must work in the fields and take care of the animals, but one needs only to buy tea, sugar, Tide, flour, and oil. God supplies the rest." *(Continued on page 235)*

Sticks for the fire, alfalfa for fodder—collecting them is women's work in the Atlas Mountains. On a ridge above the Aït Bou Guemmez, a woman goes about her task, a heavy bundle lashed to her back. Because vegetation is sparse in these denuded mountains, women must often walk several miles to find a load.

Pages 230-231: Lush barley almost ready for harvesting carpets the Aït Bou Guemmez floor beside the crumbling walls of an abandoned house. Across the valley rises a pyramidal mountain topped by a local saint's shrine, where tribesmen traditionally stored grain for safekeeping. Today pilgrims climb there to pray and make sacrifices to the saint.

Pages 232-233: Traders from the plains relax in a village restaurant during the weekly market, or souk. The men travel from valley to valley in the Atlas, their trucks brimming with goods from city factories.

"Besides," Aisha added, "the valley is improving all the time. Now we have butane gas. Someday we shall have electricity. That is all we need." For what, in particular? "Television, of course." Of course: the baraka of the modern world.

Aside from an occasional party of mountain trekkers and the vendors who haul in goods to the souk, little of the modern world has intruded on this valley. In winter heavy snows make the road impassable except by donkey or mule. One telephone line, open six hours a day, serves the valley's 8,500 people. That and half a dozen elementary schools constitute the government services. Farmers till their fields with wooden plows not seen in Europe since the Middle Ages. I had met the sole doctor, a young Frenchman, who moved here on his own initiative two years ago to become the valley's first resident doctor. Frédéric Tissot tries valiantly to cope with the infant mortality, tuberculosis, and other health problems that beset the tribe. Malnutrition, says Dr. Tissot, is the most troubling problem, and many young children die of it, not because food is lacking but because their parents feed them tea and bread, saving meat and vegetables for guests.

At Aisha's I was reminded of this as mealtime arrived. Glass after glass of intensely sweet, taste-numbing mint tea and much bantering preceded the meal. Then Aisha brought out a large platter of lamb and vegetables over steamed barley—a couscous. Four of us as guests of honor sat cross-legged at one table, and dug in after repeating *Bismillah*—In the name of God—all around, "to keep the jnun from eating with us," Aisha explained. While fighting off the scores of persistent flies, I lamely copied my companions as they scooped small handfuls of fragrant grain from the mound, tossed them in their palms until a ball formed, and then popped them into their mouths—all with a good deal of lip smacking and finger licking.

When our table had eaten its fill, the leftovers were passed on to the other guests, and Aisha pressed another steaming platter on

us. This time it was a *tajine,* a greasy stew of lamb, olives, and vegetables baked in a clay pot. And this was a meal between lunch and dinner. "Baaaaraka," I said, drawing out the first syllable as a friend had taught me to do. "Enough," it can also mean, an indispensable word in a society that puts so high a value on hospitality.

One vegetable, the potato, increasingly ties this isolated valley to the economy of modern Morocco. Truckers lumber up the steep road from Azilal during the September harvest to cut deals with the farmers. Because of the demand for Aït Bou Guemmez potatoes, many landowners are turning away from subsistence farming to allot more and more land to potatoes. They spend their newfound cash at the weekly souk on necessities they used to grow, like wheat, and sometimes on luxuries, like metal grillwork for their windows.

Muhammad Talbi, who lives near Aisha with his wife, Tuda, and four children is such a farmer. A gentle, pious man, Muhammad farms 12 small plots of land and also works in another village as a factotum to the *caid*—the government representative who took over from the tribal chief as head man in the valley. The job makes Muhammad one of only a handful of salaried workers and thus something of a bourgeois by valley standards.

I met Tuda carrying two pails of water up the path from the well. Her tall form swayed under their weight. Stop and talk, I urged. "Later," she laughed. "I have work to do." But later she had cows to milk and milk to churn and wheat to mill and bread to bake and chickens to feed and clothes to wash and spread out in the field for drying.

Toward nightfall, Muhammad relaxed with visitors on his rooftop terrace, the skirts of his *fuqiah* tucked under his legs. From our mats we could see Tuda and her oldest daughter, Fatima, slowly make their way down the nearby hillside, doubled over under enormous bundles of brush. Human brooms. Like other valley women, they collect the brush and dried alfalfa twice a day to use for the fire and as fodder in winter.

"It's not so bad. We're used to it because we do it from the age of eight," Tuda told me shyly, when she had shed her 70-pound load into a ground-floor storeroom. She brought a pot of coffee up the steep open staircase from the courtyard, pausing by the cow for several long squirts of milk. Though I begged her to stay, she quickly retreated, unaccustomed to socializing in the presence of male guests. Later I watched her crouch beside a wood fire in the kitchen, a blackened, smoke-filled, airless cell off the courtyard. I remembered Dr. Tissot telling me that many valley women suffer from tuberculosis and other respiratory diseases. How could they not?

But on the flat rooftop the air was cool and clear. Muhammad surveyed the sky, mountains, and fields arrayed before him—"the bounty that God has given," he said in Arabic, which he, like most men in the valley,

Going visiting, a favorite Aït Bou Guemmez pastime, brings out finery like this spangled wool shawl, but women weave for home consumption only. A French-Moroccan project has started to teach marketable skills to valley youths—crafts to girls and mountain guiding and beekeeping to boys.

From other Berber areas come artists to paint the ceilings of well-to-do farmers (opposite). The elaborate designs, along with rugs, banquettes, and wall hangings, decorate a room where the head of the house lavishes hospitality on guests. Other rooms may be unfinished. The host serves sweet mint tea, which women prepare in teapots over charcoal braziers sold at the souk.

can get along in. High on the surrounding slopes twinkled the fires of shepherds.

Muhammad enumerated his blessings: His children are healthy, and the crops have been excellent this year after several years of drought. And that is only the start, I could not help thinking: He has a wife and a daughter to do the work while he entertains the guests.

What about crime? I asked. "Only the foxes are thieves," Muhammad replied. "They eat the sheep and cattle. I know of no theft or murder committed here in my lifetime." Yet this is a region that used to be well known for the ferocity of its tribal warfare.

Besides the kitchen, several other rooms open off the Talbis' small courtyard: the "women's washroom," a tiny space empty except for a low stool, a sponge, and a drain; the fodder storeroom; and a room for animals right under the family's bedroom. In winter their body heat helps warm the family. Now, in good weather, the courtyard is packed with animals: two cows and their calves, a mule, several goats, and a fat sheep bought specially for Id el Kebir—the feast of sacrifice only a few days away. Then most families in the Islamic world ritually kill a sheep to commemorate Abraham's obedience to God. On the eve of the feast, the Prophet's purported near-burial place on Jebel Azourki draws scores of pilgrims from the surrounding valleys.

The feast creates a brisk market for sheep at Saturday's souk. Since long before daybreak, the clip-clop of hooves has echoed down the valley as men in djellabas, hoods raised against the chill, make their way on donkeys and mules to Tabannt, the central village. From across the mountains have come heavily laden trucks, bringing goods to the tribe from the world of modern Morocco.

Dormant six days a week, Tabannt comes alive on Saturdays, transformed by rows and rows of tents. These vendors' alleys climb several levels up the hillside. In the noisiest and liveliest, animal sellers and buyers poke, lift, examine, and bargain. Amid the din, banks of sheep and goats stand roped together. In another alley grains spill out of sacks.

Nearby, as many as 30 tents display fashions from the factories of Casablanca: lacy nylon caftans, long machine-embroidered dresses, wool djellabas, plastic shoes in bright colors. Vendors in another row sell supplies and a few foodstuffs: candles, Tide, tanks of butane, batteries, bellows, nails, Bic pens, cooking oil, tea, cones of sugar, sardines.

At the spice show around the corner, earth-colored pyramids of cumin, paprika, cinnamon, ginger, and turmeric give off their pungent scents. Vendors offer henna leaves, saddle blankets, used clothes, and large bunches of mint for tea. In an open area above the souk, butchers hang sheep and goats on hooks, slaughter them, then drag them down to skin them. They then dig out innards and carve off portions on demand. Skins and heads lie around in crumpled piles like discarded Halloween costumes.

Mouha Heddouch lives next to the souk in a stone house the French built. A tall turbaned man, his face marked by deep creases, Mouha was about nine years old in the late 1920s when a French army brigade arrived. For a while the fighting was bloody. "The valley strongly resisted," he recalls. "With the other children I was sent into the mountains for safety, but we could hear the gunfire below. Many people were killed or wounded."

Any heroes?

"One man became famous for killing French, even after they had conquered these mountains. For more than three years he went from valley to valley and from town to town picking off soldiers wherever he could find them. The French put a large bounty on his head and eventually captured and shot him. His name was Sidi Ahmed Ahansal, and he was a saint from a holy valley on the other side of Jebel Azourki."

I thought back to the hereditary saints of Talsinant, Muhammad Talbi's village, and wondered what opportunities come around these days for them to show *their* baraka.

By Elizabeth L. Newhouse
Photographs by Bruno Barbey

Ceremonial rites, conducted by married women, introduce an Aït Bou Guemmez bride to the joys and sorrows of marriage. The women perform animist rituals, such as baking bread to symbolize fertility, accompanying them with loud, joyous singing and warbling. Veiled throughout, the bride sits in the corner, her hands and feet stained with henna for happiness and luck. Amid dancing and weeping, women and girls deliver the bride to her husband's house (opposite, left). Then, with the sexes segregated, all-night feasting begins.

After the marriage is consummated, the women escort the bride to the spring to wash and drink, an Islamic rite of purification.

Pages 238-239: At the Imilchil fair, a yearly High Atlas event, marriageable women of the Aït Hadiddou tribe and eager bachelors take one another's measure. If a resulting match fails, the couple can divorce.

In New Zealand, man and dog supervise the autumn muster, moving a "mob" of sheep to lower ground.

Pastures Down Under

"**A** nation of 73 million," goes the wry New Zealand remark, "of which 70 million are sheep."

Yet time was when no mammals at all had set foot in New Zealand and its mountains. No sheep, no goats, no deer, no rabbits. None of the disastrous Australian possums. No mammals anywhere, except for two species of bats.

To see why, hold a globe at arm's length, centering it on New Zealand's two main islands. The only continents you will see are Australia and Antarctica. Almost half the world in your view, and most of it water.

New Zealand lies alone.

It has for some 70 million years, ever since Earth's slowly moving crustal plates broke it off from any continental link —before the age of mammals.

This castaway island world developed a unique ecosystem. With no four-legged carnivores, flightless birds like the kiwi and giant moa could thrive. Without hoofed herbivores, a rich variety of plant life took root beneath the trees.

Forests of fossil-like tree ferns still grow on the rain-soaked western slopes of the country's South Island, where the Southern Alps wring moisture from the prevailing westerlies. The clouds piling up along the length of the range sometimes hide all but the tallest alp, Mount Cook—hence its Maori name, Aorangi, "cloud piercer."

A Polynesian race, the Maoris arrived here in force around

A.D. 1000. They hunted out the moas, cleared some forest for farming, introduced dogs and probably rats, but made few other marks on the land. It was at least 700 years later, after the Europeans arrived and battled the Maoris to a stalemate, that the mountains changed.

In the Southern Alps, on eastern slopes too rugged and dry for the plow, the new settlers cleared the bush for huge sheep stations. Torching the land was routine. Recalling a fine burn-off around the turn of the century, W. H. Guthrie-Smith rhapsodized, "As a lover wraps his mistress in his arms, so the flames wrap the stately cabbage trees, stripping them naked of their matted mantles of brown. . . . a fire on a dry day of a dry season was worth a ride of a thousand miles." Such practices, coupled with overgrazing, would lead to decades of erosion and flooding, problems that modern land management has only begun to control.

Change comes also to the wet western side of the range. The landscape here still seems a kind of Carboniferous Eden, all mist and moss and primeval tree ferns and leaf-shrouded cascades of meltwater from the icy peaks above. Higher up, the winds drop snow, not rain. The snows feed more than 360 glaciers, some of which extend far down into the rain forest.

But these native forests face trouble. For the settlers introduced not only livestock, but wild animals, too: deer and rabbits for food and game; brush-tailed possums for fur. In an ecologically innocent age, few worried about natural predators to keep the imports in check.

The red deer destroy forest, not just by foraging, but by trampling where no being has

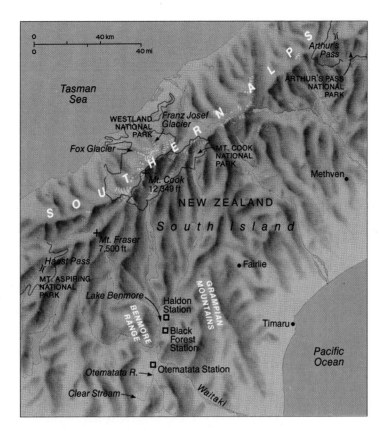

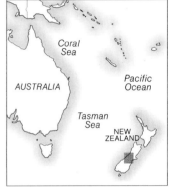

trampled before—in the delicate forest understory. Plants die, and on mountain slopes more erosion sets in. Now trappers strive to take the deer out alive, to use as breeding stock for a growing venison industry.

The prolific possums (a type of phalanger, much furrier than the American opossum) have proved even worse. They can denude entire trees by eating leaves; they destroy orchards and gardens as well as native forests. Poisoning has failed to control them.

Modern outdoor-loving New Zealanders, increasingly aware of their unique natural heritage, debate national environmental policy with vigor. The issues turn practical for people of the high country, where environmental battle means poisoning rabbits, fighting erosion, and getting the sheep down before the snows come. Yet love of land touches even the toughened sheepman. Native author Maurice Shadbolt wrote, "Familiarity, in the high country, does not breed contempt. I have seen musterers, with all of a lifetime given to the mountains, draw breath and gaze with wonder upon patterns of cloud and rock. And pause wearily in the middle of a muster to pick some alpine flower to decorate a battered hat."

By Jonathan B. Tourtellot
Photographs by
David Robert Austen

Uniquely remote, the Southern Alps run the 500-mile length of New Zealand's South Island, rising to 12,349 feet at Mount Cook. Nowhere else on Earth is such a large range so far from the nearest continent; Australia lies some 1,000 miles away.

Amid tussock grasses bronzed by autumn, a fencing crew works to enclose some of the 38,000 acres belonging to Black Forest Station, a high-country sheep ranch. Here on the dry side of the Southern Alps one sheep needs almost four acres of forage—and the station owns 10,000 head.

July snow tops hills above Lake Benmore. On its shore Black Forest Station waits through the Southern Hemisphere winter.

A mob of 500 Merino ewes heads for the paddock at Black Forest.

Self-reliance knits the fabric of station life. Field hockey for three (opposite) fills an afternoon hour at Haldon School. Following common practice on remote stations, its four students take lessons by radio. Their supervisor, Miss Siobhan Murphy—playing in blue— sends papers and tests to Wellington, the capital, for grading.

With the able help of two sons, Janet Innes of Black Forest Station makes pancakelike "pikelets," a popular midwinter treat. Two Black Forest children (left) set off through a drift of poplar leaves to help with duck hunting.

Alaska's Arrigetch Peaks soar in Gates of the Arctic National Park.

THE FAR REACHES

Tom Bean

Distant peaks, glistening with ice, awesome in beauty and in menace. . . . It is no wonder that human beings often regard these mysterious heights as the home of gods. The prophet Moses climbed Mount Sinai to commune with God, "and the Lord called unto him out of the mountain." Buddhists and Hindus alike make arduous pilgrimages to holy peaks in the Himalayas. High in the Bolivian Andes, the miners of Potosí acknowledge—and fear—the vengeful demons within the plundered mountain.

Climbers also find a spiritual meaning in lofty peaks. Mountain climbing for pleasure first became popular in the 19th century. Recent decades brought a surge of new interest. Climbers now seek ever more distant and difficult challenges, from the storm-wracked summits of Patagonia to the frigid ranges of Canada's Baffin Island, so barren and forbidding that the Inuit who live below them rarely go there.

Treasures
& Demons

Once the world's richest mountain, now a monumental pile of reddish rubble honeycombed with tunnels, Cerro Rico stands over Potosí, Bolivia, its summit 15,827 feet above sea level. Inside the extinct volcano, a crooked mile from sunlight, explosives are detonated at noonday. As with the bass of a great pipe organ, I feel more than hear their resonance in the remote recess of the mine where I am sitting on my heels eating lunch. Miners spoon potato soup out of old Klim cans by the light of lamps on their helmets. They talk about close calls with death and the devil.

"Level Nine was abandoned but the hoist kept stopping there. The operator couldn't control it."

"Following a tin vein, we accidentally drilled a hole into a gallery deserted centuries ago. We saw a miner dressed as in olden times. No helmet, no lamp, just a torch. And no face at all. He had the feet of a rooster."

My guide Edgar Alanes, secretary of the mine safety office, advises: "If you get lost and a solitary miner beckons to you from the dark of an unused tunnel, don't obey . . . for it is a demon. This is the devil's domain."

"Doesn't God have a say in here?" I ask. "I thought the devil lived in hell."

"Level Nine is hell enough."

Arguing theology in the core of a volcano was new to me but not to Potosinos caught between fantasy and fact, past and present, both beneath the ground and above it. Consider Doña Teodora, the popcorn vendor who warned me that if walking after midnight,

Silver transformed Cerro Potosí, a desolate Andean mountain, into Cerro Rico, the "hill of riches."

256

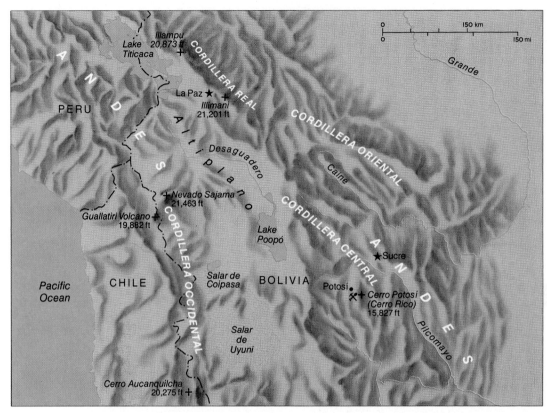

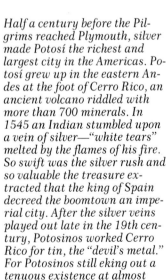

Half a century before the Pilgrims reached Plymouth, silver made Potosí the richest and largest city in the Americas. Potosí grew up in the eastern Andes at the foot of Cerro Rico, an ancient volcano riddled with more than 700 minerals. In 1545 an Indian stumbled upon a vein of silver—"white tears" melted by the flames of his fire. So swift was the silver rush and so valuable the treasure extracted that the king of Spain decreed the boomtown an imperial city. After the silver veins played out late in the 19th century, Potosinos worked Cerro Rico for tin, the "devil's metal." For Potosinos still eking out a tenuous existence at almost 14,000 feet, their city remains a remote enclave of occult beliefs.

I should keep to the middle of empty streets:

"Please, señora! In this friendly town?"

"Sí. Beware of dark alleys near San Lorenzo Church. There the ghost of Juan de Toledo sometimes appears with his skull in his hands to expiate his sin."

What sin? "In 1657 he killed his wife because he saw *un hombre fantasma* caressing her knee. Yet she was innocent; he found out too late that the phantom was the devil."

Such perceptions of the psychic netherworld are everywhere in Potosí, a town so isolated that it has few equals in the Andes as a repository of occult beliefs. But to peer into its physical depths—or at least to go down into its biggest mine, I had to request permission at COMIBOL, the government mining agency in La Paz, Bolivia's administrative capital.

Then I set out by jeep on the road to Potosí, a highway in the loftiest sense of the word: It stays above 12,000 feet elevation during the entire 357 miles from La Paz. By the second day little traffic was going my way except a herd of llamas bound for market carrying blocks of salt cut from the Coipasa salt flats.

Three or four centuries ago this road teemed with Indians, their possessions bundled in colorful woven *llicllas* on their backs. At every summit they pitched stones onto piles—still there—to give thanks for a safe journey, and blew plucked eyebrow hairs into the air as votive offerings. They were *mitayos*, an Inca word for conscript laborers brought by the Spanish from far hamlets. About 4,000 recruits a year toiled in the mines—and eventually populated the graveyards—of Potosí. Caravans of llamas bore wine and honey from the warm valleys of Peru as well as Chinese silks consigned to "Pei-tu-hsi." Men and mules carried mirrors from Flanders, paintings from Rome, coral—to cure madness—from Naples, and lodestone and jasper from shores of seas as far away as the Aegean and the Black.

In those days I might have met outbound mule trains carrying the cargo that financed those luxuries: tons of coins made of silver mined from Cerro Rico and minted in Potosí.

Night fell in a rush of frigid air just as I sighted the cone-shaped magnet that has drawn humans from all the world into these sterile heights ever since 1545, the year Diego Hualpa discovered the secret of Potosí. Hualpa, a herder from Peru, was warming himself with a fire one night when strong winds whipped the flames white hot. Molten metal oozed from a rock—the first rivulet of the silver flood to come.

By 1616, the year Cervantes and Shakespeare died, the expression in Europe for a thing of stupendous value—a royal dowry, a treasure fleet—was "It's worth a Potosí!" The city at the foot of the faraway mountain was the richest in the New World and as populous as the maritime Republic of Venice.

Among that populace, chroniclers listed 20 lawyers, 3 doctors, 10 healers, 800 gamblers, 120 prostitutes, and "300 idlers that did nothing but dress extravagantly and eat and drink to excess." There were also companies of actors, dancing teachers, and fencing masters who taught young bloods how to kill one another. Of Potosí's 160,000 inhabitants, only 3,000 were Spaniards. Nearly half were fortune seekers—Creoles, Portuguese, Italians, and Basques—obliged to work lest they be charged with vagrancy and chained to galley oars. And 76,000 were Indians.

Driven by overseers' whips, Indians dug a week at a time by torchlight in tunnels that riddled the mountaintop. Others lugged fifty-pound loads of ore up rickety rawhide ladders. Lucky were those who worked outside, tending riverside waterwheels that crushed the ore. Least fortunate of all were the Indians detailed to fire the kilns where quicksilver—used to free silver from crushed ore—was cooked off. Breathing mercury fumes led to ghastly disabilities and many deaths.

After yielding silver worth billions today, the high-grade lodes that capped the slopes diminished. By 1826 only 8,000 people lived in Potosí. But the heart of the mountain was also veined with tin, a lesser metal that haughty silver barons did not deign to mine.

"One of my ancestors pioneered the switch from silver to tin," said Juan Jorge Aitken, manager of a dairy farm in a warm valley below Potosí. "My great-grandfather Louis Soux was in the balloon business in Paris a hundred years ago when a visitor from South America, Aniceto Arce, invited him to Bolivia. Arce became the president of Bolivia and brought in a railroad from the Pacific coast. Soux married an heiress to many silver diggings of Potosí, and began to mine tin when it became profitable because of the railroad, though socially unacceptable."

But not for long. Fabulously wealthy tin kings all but ruled Bolivia until the great social revolution of 1952 threw them out. Their descendants still jet about Europe.

Now the rustle of silk is stilled in the mural-ceilinged salon of Juan Jorge's house. Violins play no longer in the balconied ballrooms of Potosí. But the chatter of woolen-shawled women in Pilgrim-like hats who sweep the streets at dawn goes on as before.

Concerned Potosinos like Filiberto Zuleta, former rector of the university, are bent on saving historic Potosí from a threatened technological onslaught. "Hydraulic engineers propose to sluice the entire volcano into the valley, recovering all sorts of ore along the way," said Señor Zuleta. "Of course the peak would live on, since its image is reproduced in the Great Seal of Bolivia and enshrined in the center of the flag."

Sluicing is limited as yet to cooperatives that truck water to tanks on the mountain, then siphon it through garden hoses to rework the tailings. I feared to enter unshored co-op tunnels, which all too often cave into one another. I preferred to tour the COMIBOL tin mine, with its 18 levels, 20 miles of tunnels, and 3 vertical (Continued on page 262)

A grinning Bacchus, god of wine, welcomes visitors to the Casa de Moneda, once the royal mint, now a museum. Its steel dies stamped out the pieces of eight coveted by pirates.

Pages 258-259: Bundled up against dawn's chill, a mestizo woman sweeps a Potosí street. Her stocky build holds warmth by reducing the area of skin where body heat can escape.

Pages 260-261: The sun's last rays warm soccer players at the base of Cerro Rico. Large lung volume and extra red blood cells supply high-altitude dwellers with additional oxygen. Enlarged capillaries boost blood flow in their hands and feet, keeping their extremities warm.

mine shafts driven down through the heart of the ancient volcano.

With my guide Edgar, I left the cool caress of sunshine and walked into the dark, icicled tunnel on Level Zero, the entrance at 13,400 feet. Edgar crossed himself and kissed his thumbnail. "Keep your hard hat on," he warned. By doing so, I suppose I escaped electrocution whenever my head banged a low-strung trolley wire.

We followed railroad tracks into the bowels of the Cerro with only headlamps to lessen the gloom. A rising reverberation stirred my fear of an earthquake. I wondered whether I carried paper enough to write good-bye notes while trapped somewhere in 20 miles of tunnels. But the rumbling was only a small electric locomotive speeding by with its train of ore cars, its operator's garish grin freeze-framed by the arcing of a trolley that he held up to the wire with a gloved hand.

In time we reached two miners filling holes with explosive charges of ammonium nitrate. I readied my cameras. The miners frowned. Photography—like women—is taboo in Bolivia's lofty mines, since it attracts *tíos* or *supayas*, mischievous demons who spoil pictures and take advantage of ladies.

Sure enough, my cold lenses kept fogging up so fast in the wet air that I finally gave up for the day. Supayas were up to their old tricks. So I planned to foil them. I told Edgar that next time I preferred to photograph miners working in "unbearable heat"—his words—1,400 feet deeper in the mine.

"Tomorrow I'll take you down to Level Eight," promised Edgar. "Not below. Not while the devil hangs out on Nine."

On the way out Edgar said some tunnels—mainly those dug secretly by would-be tin miners—so undermined the city that building foundations sometimes caved in. He pointed overhead to an unworked vein of tin. "It isn't that we failed to mine this vein. It's just that the tin wasn't there when this exploratory tunnel was dug. Minerals belong to the devil. He puts them in and steals them away from one day to the next. This lures

Pushing the limits: Though tin sustains Bolivia's economy, miners endure Dickensian conditions, whether on the tailings or inside the mine. They earn about a dollar a day and must often stop working by age 41 because of respiratory diseases.

A miner chewing coca leaves (lower left) touches up an idol of the devil; the mild narcotic helps the men endure fatigue, hunger, and cold. Before heading underground into the "devil's domain," miners leave a votive offering—a well-chewed wad of coca—at Satan's image.

Miners descend several hundred feet from Cerro Rico's icy entrance into its dark, stifling, inferno-like bowels. Stripped to loincloths and boots, they wrestle 160-pound pneumatic drills and breathe air laced with the heavy fumes of blasting powder. At shift's end the muck-coated men ride three elevators up the old volcano's throat, a trip far swifter than in colonial times, when Indians climbed rickety rawhide ladders while packing 50 pounds of ore each.

Pockmarked by four centuries of mining, Cerro Rico still holds tin, gold, copper, and a wealth of other minerals. Near an entrance on its northern slope, miners sluice tailings tinged reddish brown by oxidation. Tin is denser than rubble, so bits of tin ore, ground finer and finer by picks and shovels, settle on the bottom of the sluice, while antimony, zinc, and lighter minerals drain off the slopes into the valley below.

Millions of years ago, pods of fiery magma thrust mineral-saturated water upward from Earth's mantle and deposited precious compounds throughout Cerro Rico. Strands of silver ore, some 13 feet thick, veined the mountaintop. Most of the world's silver comes from the rumpled spine of North and South America—the Andes, Mexican Sierras, and Rockies.

men deeper and deeper into the Earth."

For a second opinion on how such a vast hoard of mineral treasure accumulated inside a single mountain, I consulted Dr. Manfred Wolf, a German geology professor teaching in Potosí. "To play along with the mind-set of your miner friends," said Dr. Wolf, "let's say that the instrument of the devil is magma underlying the Earth's surface, and yes, it is hot as hell."

Dr. Wolf explained that Cerro Rico marks the intersection of two lines of volcanoes inactive for perhaps eight million years. They formed on top of crumpled and uplifted layers of ocean sediments deposited in Paleozoic times, three or four hundred million years ago. Pods of magma under enormous pressure forced superheated water and steam into countless fractures of the Paleozoic crust. The water became saturated with dissolved minerals. Some rose up the volcanic throat of Cerro Rico, squeezed into crevices, and deposited valuable metallic compounds throughout the mountain.

"Why tin here, and silver there, or only worthless rock?" Dr. Wolf's eyes twinkled. "The demons know better than I."

To foil the supayas, I kept my cameras and lenses wrapped up with hot water bottles next day as I entered the wet heat of Level Eight. Walking in with the added weight, I tired quickly. There is 30 percent less oxygen in every breath at 13,400 feet.

At a vertical hoist lodged in the throat of the old volcano, a cage took us down 800 feet in 20 seconds. The temperature shot up just as fast. Edgar and I stripped down to swimming trunks, stuffed cotton in our ears, and entered a tunnel walled with sparkling iron pyrites. It got hotter with every step.

In this confined space the jackhammering of a compressed-air drill sounded like warfare. Two operators were chipping rock and ore out of the heart of Cerro Rico. The men worked nearly naked in gray muck under a spray from the hose cooling the drill bit.

Withdrawing to a cavern, I spread a shower curtain over thick mud to ready my gear.

My thermometer read 32°C (90°F). Sweat muddied my eyeballs with dust from the drilling. Despite the humidity the warm camera lenses did not fog; I had foiled the supayas. I started shooting.

Muck spewing from the drill raised hell with my equipment. Focusing by lamplight was uncertain. My arms and legs weighed tons. Tiring fast, I breathed deeply to restore oxygen to my blood. Oddly, I felt worse with every breath. Was I succumbing to acute altitude sickness for the first time in my life? Rather embarrassing, since both miners apparently felt fine.

Inhaling air from a hissing rupture in the drill's hose kept me going a little longer. But slowly I slid from reality into a noisy nightmare and sank into the slop. . . .

. . . I came to, half dressed, bathed in sweat, lying alone in an infirmary with blood-stained walls on Level Zero. A paramedic brought me a sip of coca-leaf tea and a soiled aspirin tablet. I listened to distant voices. ". . . supayas trip up photographer . . . gases got to the gringo . . . three days ago a miner collapsed on Level Eight . . . asphyxiated . . . carbon monoxide gas. . . ."

Carbon monoxide! Could that be why I got dizzy when hyperventilating? Once the lethal gas gets into the blood and displaces oxygen, it cannot be quickly breathed away—and can lead to death by asphyxiation.

Why weren't the miners affected? A lifetime of adaptation? Fresh air from the drill rig blowing in their faces? Or circumstances too esoteric for me to fathom?

After a while an ore train whisked me out of the mine and into the healing light of the sun that the Incas in their high Andean kingdom once worshiped with such good reason.

I sent word that I'd left a roll of film at the end of the tunnel near the drill site.

Word came back that the film was gone—and that under the shower curtain where I'd laid out my equipment, there were giant rooster footprints in the mud.

Text and photographs by Loren McIntyre

Under the gutted cone of Cerro Rico, dusk brings to Potosí's ghostly streets an illusion of long-vanished grandeur. Just after the winter solstice, on the eve of St. John's Day, bonfires (lower right) blaze in the streets and countryside, illuminating one of the longest, coldest nights of the year in a plea for the renewed fertility of fields and flocks. It is said that grain will grow as high as a person can leap over the flames.

By day Aymara musicians play sampoñas, or reed panpipes, on Potosí's streets. Conquistadores called the music "devilish," complaining that the shrill tunes curdled their "blood with horror." Men knit their own caps, whose colors and motifs tell where a person is from.

Her jaunty derby hat shows that the popcorn vendor, who sells bags of puffed corn, wheat, and rice, is an Aymara-speaking chola, or mestizo woman. Bolivia's cholas mind the stores and market stalls, working hard at jobs their society deems unworthy of men.

In the Land Beyond Summer

The pilot would never return to his light plane, left parked out at the airstrip, but no one knew that yet.

I had just missed meeting him, they said in the settlement of Broughton Island; he had decided to make the 60-mile hike through the mountains to Pangnirtung, and planned to fly back on the commercial plane next week. He was from the South—here in Baffin "South" means Toronto or Montreal or any place one or two thousand miles toward summer—and he wanted to experience spectacular Pangnirtung Pass before going home.

The Inuit of Broughton thought nothing of it. Every summer a few *qallunaat,* as Inuit call all those forceful, restless people who live in the South, come here to hike through the pass or climb a few icy mountains. That they do so is accepted, if not understood. After all, there is no game to speak of up in the mountains. No seal, no walrus, no narwhal, no char. Even the caribou that flee to the highlands to escape the summer mosquitoes do not go very high, for there is nothing up there but rock and ice. The Inuit prefer to be here, along the rugged coast created by the meeting of mountains and sea. Here amid the fiords and bluffs and inlets and ice floes there is game, and the weather is better. No one lives inland.

Perhaps that is why this chain of mountains, so long that it could reach from Nova Scotia to Florida, has no name. It runs from

David L. Brill

In Canada's Auyuittuq National Park Reserve a mountainside rises above the glacier that helped carve it.

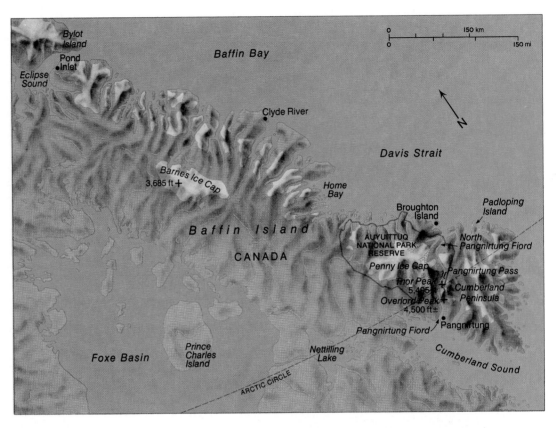

Erosion has whittled the uplifted northeast coast of 1,000-mile-long Baffin Island into an icy, rugged tangle of fiords, islands, and barren mountains.

Without the life-giving seas at the base of these peaks, people would no more live here than atop Mount Kenya, for climatically all the Arctic is a mountaintop, far above the Northern Hemisphere's tree line. So the island's few inhabitants—mainly Inuit—live by the water, where they can hunt seal and other game. Six of Baffin's nine lonely settlements lie on the mountainous side of the island, where the rugged coast offers better shelter and hunting than the flat, exposed shore and shallow sea on the southwestern side.

Ellesmere Island, on the Arctic Ocean, southeastward for 1,700 miles, tapering off in the Torngat of northern Labrador. Where gaps in the chain are broad and deep enough, ocean flows in, forming straits that cut the land into islands—Ellesmere, Devon, and Baffin, the largest. Baffin Island straddles the Arctic Circle. It is the fifth largest island in the world, bigger than the state of California. Fewer than 8,000 people live there.

Most are Inuit—as Eskimos prefer to call themselves. In Inuktitut, their language, *inuit* simply means "people"; *inuk* is a person.

A few qallunaat live in Baffin too, some lured by the same stark grandeur that beckoned the pilot now making his way through the pass. Those who settle here must brave the rigors of a land where no crops grow, where the nearest tree may be 500 miles to the south, where camping means going

armed in case of polar bear attack, and where winter temperatures can easily dive to 50 below. One southern transplant marveled to me about the exhilarating, scary landscape. "It's huge. It weighs on the mind, it's so huge. And then you look at the Inuit hunters who go out into the land all the time and are so stoic about it—." He shook his head.

Here around Broughton, between breakup and freeze-up, when you can go for days without frost, those hunters use outboard-powered freighter canoes to roam the rugged Baffin coastline. I have taken a week this August to go out "on the land" with two of them.

Cruising slowly, Jonas Audlakiak scans the water in the steep-walled fiord. Beside him the boy Juelie does the same. The big canoe floats on a mirror of gray mountainside, a glassy calm perfect for hunting.

Juelie cries out. One or two hundred feet

away a furry head pokes out above the water. The teenager grabs a well-worn rifle, fires. The head disappears. The two Inuit resume watching, unperturbed. The first shot usually misses. The idea is to shoot before the seal can get a full breath, and so force it to resurface more often. In winter it's different; you wait on the ice at the floe edge or at the seal's breathing hole, rifle aimed. Maybe for hours.

The head reappears, now off to the right. Juelie fires again. Another miss. But the seal had little time to draw air. A few more tries and a shot connects. Jonas guns the boat forward and Juelie gaffs the carcass before it can sink. *Natsiq,* a ringed seal. He hangs the head over the side of the stern so the blood will flow overboard. The wake turns crimson.

On the rocky shore of a rocky hump called Padloping Island they butcher the kill, eating the tenderloin raw. To my qallunaat palate it tastes bloody, but tender indeed. After dining on the liver and ribs, they fold the skin carefully and stow it aboard the boat.

"How much will you get for the skin, Jonas?" "Three dollars, maybe five dollars." Less than an hour's gas for the outboard. Once it was $45, back before the qallunaat world stopped buying much sealskin.

But who can understand the ways of the qallunaat? They spew questions, instead of watching patiently, Inuit style. They knock at your door and make you come to open it, instead of just walking in. They insist on fixed mealtimes. They climb mountains. And always they bring changes. They brought rifles and a cash economy, and snowmobiles and outboard motors, and satellite TV.

An Inuit elder had told me of his first meeting with the white strangers and their devices. It was right here on Padloping, more than 70 years ago, when he was a boy. A ship appeared, and pale-faced men rowed in from it to pay a visit to his family's camp. "They gave us a box of matches. We didn't have a clue what it was, so we threw the matches in the water and kept the box." He chuckled. Now he lives in one of the settlements the qallunaat built and asked the Inuit to move

Jonathan B. Tourtellot, National Geographic Staff

into, so that the children could go to school.

But people still like to go out on the land, camping as we are. I begin to see why. Your senses fill with the Arctic: the steely touch of clean air on your cheek; the taste of campfire tea; an iceberg's shocking blue-white amid soft earth tones of lichen and tundra and stone; and silence so deep it enframes each tiny sound—the croak of a distant raven, the crunch of gravel underfoot, the clunk inside your skull of your own teeth meeting.

The bluffs of Padloping dwindle behind the canoe. In the long twilight we head back to Broughton, aiming the prow into the thudding swell and the face-numbing wind, and arrive in darkness and cold, when ghost-rivers of mist flow into the fiords.

The plane from Broughton to Pangnirtung flies right over the scenery that may lure some qallunaat dollars back to the North. I'm

Within yards of the Arctic Circle, hikers mount a mossy slope high above Pangnirtung Pass in Auyuittuq. The craterlike lake below formed where a glacier left an arc of moraine. Increasingly, refugees from more populous climes fly north on a pilgrimage to solitude amid these stark mountainscapes.

Pages 272-273: A sunburst in May augurs months of endless daylight in Pangnirtung Pass. Low on the distant horizon, hook-shaped Thor Peak soars almost a mile above the valley. Scientist-explorers in the 1950s bestowed Norse names on peaks here to honor tenth-century Vikings, the first Europeans known to see Baffin's coast.

Stephen J. Krasemann, DRK Photo

274

His freighter canoe safely moored, an Inuit hunter enjoys a treat to repel nonarctic eyes: raw liver of ringed seal, still warm. The name "Eskimo" is widely believed to come from an Indian term for "eaters of raw meat." So they are—but many Inuit, suspecting the Indians did not intend flattery, prefer their own native name.

The traditional Inuit diet— little more than fish and meat —is surprisingly nutritious. Since World War II, though, Inuit health has suffered from the import of appealing but less nutritious processed foods. Now some experts promote a return to native "country food," which provides hefty doses of vitamin C from such sources as maktaq *(whale skin) and seal liver—provided they are eaten raw.*

David L. Brill

lucky; I get a seat. This turboprop airliner is taxi, school bus, delivery truck, and ambulance for the Baffin coast. You fly if the weather's fair, if the plane isn't needed for a Medivac run, if the teenagers from Pond Inlet who must travel 700 miles down-island to board at the high school in Frobisher Bay left any seats. Otherwise, you wait a few days.

From the window you can watch in comfort as the peaks of Auyuittuq National Park Reserve slide by below. Beyond, the Penny Ice Cap smothers the mountain jumble in white smoothness, hence the name Auyuittuq, "land that never melts." The park, one of Canada's wildest, draws a trickle of the adventurous. At least a dozen are down there below me right now, including the airman from Broughton. Despite official warnings about avalanches, glacial torrents, August snow squalls, rockslides, and howling rainstorms, some hikers—like him—go in alone.

Lift your gaze from the threatening wildness below and you see a strangely even horizon. No peak out-towers the next. You could set a tabletop on them.

The reason lies 60 million years in the past, when this land swelled into a bulge more than a mile high and over 1,500 miles long, and then split like the crust of baking bread. Greenland was leaving North America.

Ocean filled the widening rift, to become Baffin Bay and Davis Strait. Wind and wave and rain went to work on the high escarpment where the sundered tableland met the new sea. Ice age glaciers carved and gouged, eating back into the highlands and digging U-shaped valleys one mile, two miles down. And when the ice sheets melted and the valleys filled with seawater to become fiords, left behind was the rock that resisted erosion: great peaks of it, mountains not raised from below but scooped out from the top down.

The glacier-carved walls of Pangnirtung Fiord fill the window as the plane descends to the airstrip. Along the strip a chain link fence sports several sealskins stretched out to dry.

Passengers step off into a stiff breeze— calm for Pangnirtung, which is so windy that

In a newsprint-insulated camp on Cumberland Sound, a woman scrapes blubber from a sealskin with her *ulu,* the all-purpose knife customarily used only by females. Sealskin once earned most of the cash needed for modern supplies that the Inuit have come to rely on: bullets, gasoline, snowmobiles, tea, and clothes from the local Hudson's Bay Company store. But in the 1970s a worldwide furor arose over the way non-Inuit hunters were clubbing baby harp seals in far-off Newfoundland. People stopped buying sealskin, regardless of source, age, or species. The bewildered Inuit found their livelihood gone. Now they sell skins for low, government-subsidized prices, and draw welfare.

David L. Brill

David L. Brill

Fred Bruemmer

houses must be lashed to the rock with steel cables over their roofs. Traders picked this spot, in 1921; the Inuit rarely camped in such exposed places. But when the settlement program began, officials were thinking of airstrip sites, not the logic of tradition.

Pangnirtung turns out to be no uglier than most arctic towns, where junk with no place to go piles up between the shabby buildings. Trash abounds. This society, whose garbage was biodegradable just a generation ago, has yet to learn antilitter habits. In a climate where an empty Coke can may last for millennia the future looks even messier than it does southward, whence the litter came.

The town is a staging area for Auyuittuq, and some residents profit from park tourism by ferrying hikers 20 miles up the fiord to the trailhead campsite beneath Overlord Peak.

A few Inuit become park wardens. For the first time an Inuk can find work *in* the mountains. One warden sees possibilities: "I want to start a cross-country ski club for the young people. Many young people in Pangnirtung have nothing to do. I want to help them learn to live from backpacks. With the park here there will be a need for more guides."

With one frozen prize shouldered, fishermen trek homeward with a catch of arctic char. Fish and sea mammals represent two main types of country food, caribou the third. To aid in stalking caribou, hunters have for centuries used rock cairns, or inukshuks, shaped enough like a man to spook the animals into running whichever way their pursuers wanted.

Pages 278-279: Thousands of years worth of snowfall packed into an icy, flowing mass—a glacier—scrapes its way from the Penny Ice Cap down into the sea. Climatologists watch Baffin Island's ice for signs of change. The Barnes and Penny Ice Caps probably represent the very last of the great Laurentide Ice Sheet that once covered half of North America. When the next continental ice age begins, many experts think, it will begin here.
David L. Brill

280   Yet, like so much in Baffin, the new work is risky. The unforgiving mountains can undo even the hardy Inuit. A local elder, Etoangat, told me of a shaman whose family was starving one winter long ago. The shaman sent her husband through a nearby pass to seek help. "The husband never made it. I saw his skull in the pass. It's probably still there."

That tale echoes in the mind when bits and pieces of rumor begin to fly around town: *Some guy hurt in the park . . . turned up alone at Overlord, chilled, wet, limping . . . not sure why . . . some campers fed him, warmed him up . . . radioed the wardens, but they had to wait for the morning tide. . . .*

. . . When they got there, he was dead.

It would be weeks before the autopsy report: heart failure "due to stress from hypothermia"—to which the wardens would add "hiking alone." He was 42, and a pilot.

Given its rigors, Auyuittuq has a fine park safety record. And yet these mountains kill so casually—easy as taking a walk.

So it is good, now as I gaze up to where a new dawn outlines Overlord, to have Harry Dialla and July Papatsie hiking in with me. Both men are wardens.

As we ready our packs, the air suddenly roars with what sounds like a jet coming in low. *Here?* I search the sky, almost overlooking the cloud of dust rising from a slope up the pass. Rockslide! Safely distant, but a reminder of how violent this landscape can be. The glaciers retreated from these valleys only about 8,000 years ago, and the walls are still eroding into stability.

As you hike into the pass, you see no plant life anchoring those slopes. Tundra, bright with autumn, lies only in the valleys. Above soar cliffs inlaid with thin waterfalls, and pinnacles entwined with mist.

What you do see, day after day, are rocks. Rocks fallen from cliffs, rocks dropped by glaciers, rocks bulldozed into moraines, rocks bigger than houses, rocks balanced on other rocks. No wonder the Norse seafarers who sighted the layered rock of Baffin's coast named it Helluland, Land of Flat Stones.

Andy Pruna

An airplane wings into Pangnirtung Fiord, gateway to the Auyuittuq National Park Reserve, where some Inuit now find jobs as park wardens. For search-and-rescue work they must learn rock climbing, despite a historical distaste for heights. Inuit mountaineering once meant no more than scrambling up cliffs after seabird eggs, such as those of the black guillemot (right). Said one young warden of his skill: "It's something new for the people up here. My father was typical. He wouldn't even go on top of a house. When we were kids we had to sneak away to do some rock climbing, and we had to keep it quiet." New ways for old; like the land, the Inuit change but endure.

Fred Bruemmer

David L. Brill

On the rocks grow lichens, black and green. The size of a green lichen tells its age; just multiply the diameter in inches by 1,000 years, then subtract 600. Here's a specimen, three inches wide. It predates Rome.

Look up-valley and the rocks are dark with lichen growth. But face down-valley and they are scoured clean by blowing sand and snow. Katabatic winds—downdrafts of chilled air—pour off the Penny Ice Cap and add to the blasts that often funnel through the pass. At times you can barely stand up in the gusts.

On our last day we head back, following a trail marked by the stone cairns the Inuit call *inukshuks*. Harry says different types of inukshuks used to mean different things—"meat stored here," "sheltered cove," "caribou"—and a different word described each. "But I don't remember many of them." Neither does July. They readily admit that much of their culture is disappearing. That is why, after the sealskin market collapsed, the Inuit could not simply return to the old subsistence ways, ways unknown to a generation raised in settlements. July, only 24 himself, says, "Young kids know how to speak the general words of Inuktitut, but a lot of them don't know the words that are used out on the land in hunting, or the names for certain seasons or winds or snowdrifts. All that is being lost."

Still, such basics as fall caribou hunting go on: Load the family, a tent, some tea and pilot biscuits into the boat and head out for a few days on the land. I once joined a group near Pond Inlet in Baffin's far north. A half dozen families had set up their canvas tents on a fiord, deep inland. Three parties found caribou that day, one man tracking his prey long into the bright twilight. A child long grown might recall such an evening: After the feasts, while adults debated outboard motor repair, you would play outside with the other children, stalking each other, playing life and death among tents aglow with Coleman light beneath the blue-black sky and shadowy mountainsides of your true home: the land.

By Jonathan B. Tourtellot

The Realm of the Gods

Three figures trudged beneath a dome of cobalt skies. The winter snow, now in August, retreated up the lead gray scree slopes. Blinding sunlight reflected off the north-facing Himalayan crests, where the snow never leaves. Not a voice nor the cry of a bird cracked the purity of silence. Only the rasp of our labored breath and the crunch of our boots filled the air.

Eric Valli and I had come with Karma, a young man from the village of Shimen, to learn the ways of Dolpo, one of the last traditional Tibetan cultures. The 4,700 Dolpo-pa live in northwestern Nepal in some of the highest inhabited valleys in the world. From Pokhara, seven hours by bus west of Kathmandu, we had set out on foot. Now, on the tenth day, we climbed steadily for five hours to the 16,500-foot pass, Mo La.

"*Bistare janus didi*—Go slowly, Sister," Karma called.

Impatient to reach the easternmost village of Dolpo before nightfall, I ignored him and skidded down the slippery slope. In the shadows cast by the dying sunlight, Charkha resembled a medieval fortress, the inward canted stone walls of its houses rising from the embankment. Spiny piles of juniper branches, stored on the roofs for fuel, crowned the tiny-windowed houses.

We pitched camp on the edge of Charkha,

The village of Charkha commands the Barbung River Valley in Dolpo, northwestern Nepal.

284

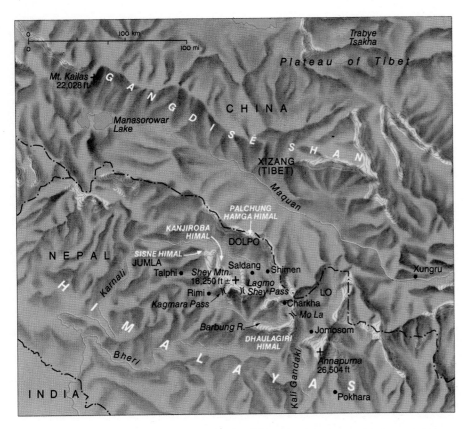

In a horseshoe of Himalayan peaks lies the land of Dolpo, the Nepalese home of the Dolpo-pa, people of Tibetan culture. Every year the Dolpo-pa cross the Himalayan ranges along ancestral caravan trails.

Above were a living area and a roof terrace. Linking the floors as ladders were notched tree trunks that had traveled on yak-back from the pine forests to the south.

We stepped through a low doorway into the darkness of the stable. The smell of hay blended with the warm animal smells of the sheep and goats and the sweet milkiness of a *dri*—a female yak. My fingers guided me along the rough stone wall as I followed the sound of Pema's footsteps across the stable and up the ladder. The glow of smoldering embers on the hearth and a shaft of sunlight from the ventilation hole in the soot-hung ceiling were the only illumination. There were no windows in the 10-by-12-foot room. In Dolpo, night temperatures during the seven-months winter drop to 20° below zero.

Pema gestured us to seats at the hearth. To our right, a man sat spinning wool on a distaff. He explained that he was Pema's husband, named Nyima because Nyima means Sunday, the day that he was born. His bright, almond-shaped eyes sparkled and a gap-toothed smile flashed as he talked.

He too wore a necklace. From the waistband that gathered his sooty, smoke-odorous, once-white chuba hung a silver-sheathed dagger and a tinder pouch of yak leather studded with turquoise and edged with silver. Nyima seemed a man of some wealth.

Two blue-and-white Chinese porcelain bowls lay by the hearth. Spitting into each, Pema wiped them clean with the hem of her apron and filled them with a handful of roasted, ground barley, or tsampa, a pat of yak butter, and shavings of dry cheese. She poured in a little tea to moisten everything. Imitating Pema, I kneaded the ingredients with my right hand, and Pema laughed at the spilled tsampa in my lap. When I had molded a ball of the mixture—*pak*—I popped it into my mouth. It tasted like raw pastry.

While we chatted, Pema nursed her baby, the youngest of eight she had borne. Three had died during infancy. Pema had tied cowrie shells into the baby's hair, and sewed a row of them across the back of his jacket. If

accompanied by chattering, giggling, grimy children. Layers of dirt caked clothing, faces, hair, legs. Their ragged clothes smelled of smoke, their skin like the earth. It was as if they had been born out of the soil.

In the morning, Pema, a village woman, came to our camp to ask if we wanted to buy potatoes to supplement our rations. Deep wrinkles lined her friendly, round, brown face. She wore a sleeveless black coat, or *chuba,* a striped apron, woolen pants tucked into her boots, and a necklace of coral and amber chunks. Also on her throat bulged a goiter the size of a tennis ball, evidence of her iodine-poor diet from crops grown in the glacially leached soils.

We followed Pema back through the maze of pathways that wound between the houses. Like the other 40 houses of Charkha, hers had a ground floor for animals and storage.

Born from its world of stone, a monastery stands below the folded layer upon layer of ancient seabeds—strata that count the oceans that repeatedly covered the Himalayan region millions of years ago.

The people of Dolpo follow a religion of Buddhism colored by animism. For the Dolpo-pa, divinity resides in the earth, air, forests, streams, especially in the mountains themselves. Every village has its god who lives in a palace inside the mountain and wears jewels and fine silk clothes. Some gods are always malicious; others wreak vengeance if a Dolpo-pa fails to ask the god's permission to plow, sow, harvest, build a house, commence a journey, or to undertake any activity that intrudes upon the god's domain.

Some 4,700 Dolpo-pa live in this 600-square-mile region of arid, rugged valleys 12,000 to 14,000 feet high. The Dolpo-pa maintain a delicate balance of life by raising yaks, goats, and sheep, cultivating barley, and trading.

demons came to steal the baby's life force, his spirit would hide in the shells.

Pema told the story of Shey, Dolpo's most sacred mountain. In the legendary past, a fierce god ruled Dolpo, and the people worshiped the spirits of the soil, the streams, and the mountains. A Tibetan lama rode on a flying snow lion to battle the mountain deity and conquered him. Then the lama changed the god into a mountain of pure crystal—Shey means "crystal" in Tibetan.

As the auspicious time of August's full moon approached, Pema and Nyima invited us to join them and Nyima's brother Renzing on the pilgrimage to Shey, made every year by the faithful to earn religious merit.

Our trail wound northwestward through rolling hills. A soft drizzle fell from the overcast skies, and the mountains rose into gray clouds. Low growths of bush honeysuckle and juniper, tufts of grass, and the white blossoms of edelweiss carpeted the landscape. The mountain range to our right traced the Chinese border.

We kept pace with the grazing yaks, from three to ten miles a day. At night we pitched our nylon tents among the black yak-hair tents. The yaks sniffed around inquisitively, tripping over the tent ropes in the dark.

These sturdy bovines are crucial to the Dolpo-pa. The dri's milk adds protein to their diet in cheese and yogurt. People eat the meat. Tibetan tea cannot be made without yak butter. The butter fuels household and votive lamps, and protects skin against sun and wind. From yak hair, men and women weave bags, tents, ropes, blankets. The hide provides leather for boot soles. The best fuel in Dolpo is yak dung. Yaks are draft animals and beasts of *(Continued on page 290)*

Born from its world of stone, a monastery stands below the folded layer upon layer of ancient seabeds—strata that count the oceans that repeatedly covered the Himalayan region millions of years ago.

The people of Dolpo follow a religion of Buddhism colored by animism. For the Dolpo-pa, divinity resides in the earth, air, forests, streams, especially in the mountains themselves. Every village has its god who lives in a palace inside the mountain and wears jewels and fine silk clothes. Some gods are always malicious; others wreak vengeance if a Dolpo-pa fails to ask the god's permission to plow, sow, harvest, build a house, commence a journey, or to undertake any activity that intrudes upon the god's domain.

Some 4,700 Dolpo-pa live in this 600-square-mile region of arid, rugged valleys 12,000 to 14,000 feet high. The Dolpo-pa maintain a delicate balance of life by raising yaks, goats, and sheep, cultivating barley, and trading.

demons came to steal the baby's life force, his spirit would hide in the shells.

Pema told the story of Shey, Dolpo's most sacred mountain. In the legendary past, a fierce god ruled Dolpo, and the people worshiped the spirits of the soil, the streams, and the mountains. A Tibetan lama rode on a flying snow lion to battle the mountain deity and conquered him. Then the lama changed the god into a mountain of pure crystal—Shey means "crystal" in Tibetan.

As the auspicious time of August's full moon approached, Pema and Nyima invited us to join them and Nyima's brother Renzing on the pilgrimage to Shey, made every year by the faithful to earn religious merit.

Our trail wound northwestward through rolling hills. A soft drizzle fell from the overcast skies, and the mountains rose into gray clouds. Low growths of bush honeysuckle and juniper, tufts of grass, and the white blossoms of edelweiss carpeted the landscape. The mountain range to our right traced the Chinese border.

We kept pace with the grazing yaks, from three to ten miles a day. At night we pitched our nylon tents among the black yak-hair tents. The yaks sniffed around inquisitively, tripping over the tent ropes in the dark.

These sturdy bovines are crucial to the Dolpo-pa. The dri's milk adds protein to their diet in cheese and yogurt. People eat the meat. Tibetan tea cannot be made without yak butter. The butter fuels household and votive lamps, and protects skin against sun and wind. From yak hair, men and women weave bags, tents, ropes, blankets. The hide provides leather for boot soles. The best fuel in Dolpo is yak dung. Yaks are draft animals and beasts of *(Continued on page 290)*

burden—without them there would scarcely be a barley crop or a caravan.

On the seventh morning we saw Shey Mountain, with its sparkling veins of quartz. Below it, at a river junction, a dozen houses clustered around a large building daubed with red ocher to mark it as a *gompa*—a temple. A hundred pilgrims from all over Dolpo were camped at Shey. Inside the tents, people sat cross-legged around small fires, exchanging news: Children have married; a wolf killed a horse; someone has brought raw wool to barter. The rain continued and the full moon gave a silver light.

In the early morning dark, the pilgrims prepared for the ritual ten-mile walk around Shey Mountain. People made breakfast of tea and tsampa. They cooked thick cakes of buckwheat, and mixed pak to carry inside the folds of their chubas. On the trail, they walked briskly, though the ground was slippery after the rain.

Everyone dressed in their best. The women were shawled in brightly striped blankets. Clusters of tiny brass bells on their waistbands tinkled with the quick steps. Those who had them wore turquoise, amber, coral, ivory, and silver. Poorer women wore plastic beads and red and green glass bangles. The older men and women clasped wooden rosaries. As they paced, they murmured prayers.

We followed a narrow trail along a stream for two hours, then began a steep climb, the line of people stretching more than half a mile. Some of the younger pilgrims chased one another, their laughter echoing through the canyon. People paused at sacred sites along the way. At the base of a cliff, pilgrims scratched at the friable clay, then ate the powder, believing it a universal benediction. Near the end of the canyon they queued to drink at a regenerating spring.

Above 16,000 feet, fresh snow dusted the path to the shrine of the goddess Drolma. Prostrate pilgrims touched their foreheads to the ground. At a cairn, masts held hundreds of prayer flags whipping in the icy blasts. Some bore the image of (Continued on page 297)

The stone houses of Dolpo have corrals for nighttime protection of animals. Women weave and chat in the corrals, shielded from icy winds. By firelight Tschewang sews boots of yak leather. On the shelf beside him are the horns of a dead yak, his favorite. On the horns he has carved a sacred motto in gratitude for the yak's service during life. The essential yak carries burdens; the female dri also provides milk on caravan —where women paint their faces with a mixture of roots as a sun shade.

Pages 286-287: Winnowing barley with her companions, a woman whistles (far left) to summon the wind that blows the chaff from the grain.

Pages 288-89: Precious willows are among the rare trees in northern Dolpo. Near Shimen stand tents of Tibetan nomads who will trade salt and wool for the yak butter and barley of the Dolpo-pa. Barley, piled high, waits for threshing. It will be spread on the ground as villagers in two lines alternately beat it with long-handled flails. On sunny autumn days, the valley resounds with the singing of workers and the rhythmical thwack, thwack, thwack, thwack of the flails.

With the waning of every year comes migration to lower villages on the southern flanks of the Himalayas. Here Dolpo-pa trade salt for grain in an exchange centuries old. On the caravan trail, grandmother Chiring and grandson rest in camp. Two Dolpo-pa, Tilen and Ongdi, brew the fortifying broth-like Tibetan tea with salt and yak butter. Within a rampart of salt bags that protects them from the wind, a family prepares dinner of barley and dried yak meat. A Dolpo family counts its wealth in houses and fields, in yaks, and in jewelry worn by both men and women—coral and amber necklaces, ivory bracelets, silver amulet boxes to carry written prayers, and Mao badges from Tibetan traders.

Pages 292-293: Yaks climb to Kagmara, "the pass where crows die," at some 17,000 feet. Each animal carries as much as 180 pounds of salt.

Pages 294-295: Caravaners camp at sunset by the river that leads them southward to their destination.

Diane Summers

the horse of the wind, who would carry their prayers to the goddess.

By early evening we had returned to camp and gathered around a fire to share bowls of *chang*—barley beer. To the strumming of a *dramyan,* a five-string Himalayan lute, some thirty pilgrims formed a ring around the blazing hearth, men on one side, women on the other. They circled, four steps toward the fire, four steps back, the rhythm quickening toward the end of each tune. Eric and I linked arms with the dancers to imitate their pounding steps. Faces and jewelry glimmered in the firelight.

The families of Dolpo move again, with their animals, every November. Their crops, grown with irrigation, can sustain them for no more than eight months of each year. Survival depends on barter and transhumance. For hundreds of years they gathered for winter grazing in southwestern Tibet. After the Chinese occupation of Tibet, in 1959, political tensions ended that, and the Dolpo-pa turned to the valleys of southern Nepal.

Renzing had promised that we could travel with him. His wife, Chiring, met us at their home in Saldang. As she ground roasted barley on a stone hand mill, Chiring told us, "Soon we will leave for the land of the grain."

Villagers prepared for the journey. Men sewed new soles to their family's boots and mended the striped woolen bags that hold the salt to be traded for grain. Other Dolpo-pa repaired the wooden packsaddles and made ropes to secure the loads. The women ground barley for tsampa. Children went into the mountains to gather brush and yak dung as winter fuel for villagers like Renzing's mother, Dawa, who was too frail to make the trip.

People held ceremonies to ensure a successful journey. The village lama came to the roof terrace of Renzing and Chiring's house. His deep red chuba flapped against his legs in the cold wind as he blew on a conch shell to call the gods to the feast. The ceremonial cakes—small cones molded from tsampa and chang—were ready beside butter lamps and a plate of barley grain. Fragrant juniper

smoldered on a flat stone. The lama sat cross-legged, rattled a drum, and murmured prayers. Chiring brought bowls of chang to the lama and Renzing.

"*Lha gyalo*—the gods of the skies are victorious!" Renzing cried as he hung new prayer flags. The lama flicked drops of chang to the four sacred directions, and tossed small handfuls of barley into the air as offerings to the gods of the mountains. From the prayer-flag poles, ravens swooped for the grain.

On the day of the full moon, 50 yaks and dri stood in Renzing's field. Renzing and his son Sonam hobbled the yaks, and Chiring, with her oldest daughter, Yesangmo, held the horns of the nervous animals while the men loaded them with salt, cooking pots, blankets, food, and other household goods.

Her old body bent, Dawa came to bid us farewell. Into our hands she pressed gifts of dried yak cheese and wizened apricots. On our heads she placed a dab of butter—for a safe journey. We touched foreheads with Dawa as a token of respect.

Tinkling bells and excited chatter filled the morning air as our caravan left Saldang. Renzing and Sonam whistled sharply to encourage the yaks. Chiring and her daughters walked at the rear with a flock of goats. The yaks, goats, and families of Renzing's neighbors, Tilen and Lhundrup, walked ahead, churning the dry soil into dust.

The flow of people and animals swelled at every crossroad. A tired child rode astride a pony led by his mother. The loads borne by the yaks creaked against the packsaddles. Snorting and panting, the yaks labored toward Lagmo Shey Pass.

At dusk we camped. The men chanted soothingly to the yaks as they unloaded. "Up there, you spotted yak, stop.... Two black yaks over there, don't fight.... You with the white horns, don't stray."

Inside a shelter of piled-up salt bags, we gathered around the fire. Voices rose and fell and the smells of smoke and sweat hung in the air. Chiring cooked a bubbling stew of dried yak meat and tsampa. A pot of buttered

The caravan ascends Kagmara Pass, 11 days into their journey and two days from their goal in Rimi, where they winter. The Dolpo-pa also trade in the valleys of Jumla. The strain of labor marks the face of a heavily burdened girl. Every year some 400 people make the crossing with hundreds of sheep and goats and a thousand yaks. Because yaks have few sweat glands and very heavy coats, they do not thrive below 10,000 feet.

300

tea warmed on the coals. Renzing smacked his lips in anticipation, but before drinking he flicked drops of tea into the air, calling to the gods, "Please take!"

After dinner, Sonam played his dramyan and improvised a song about old Angyal of Ringmo, who was too lazy to mend his boots. In a snowstorm on the way back from Tibet, the soles fell off and Angyal's toes turned black. The family burst into laughter. Then, as the fire faded, everyone crawled between warm sheepskins. With her head pillowed on a sweet-smelling bag of tsampa, Chiring drifted toward sleep.

pptt . . . pptt . . . pptt . . . Renzing spit softly. *. . . pptt . . . pptt . . . pptt . . .* Sonam spit. Chiring woke and started spitting, and nudged her sleepy daughters. "A shooting star crossed the sky," she told them. "It brings the demons. You must spit to get rid of the bad luck."

When Renzing's head emerged the next morning, it was almost zero, and last night's bowl of tea lay frozen by his head. This was a rest day, but the following morning we set out again. As we descended, the barren, gray mountain world became green with pine forests and blue with the lake waters. On the eleventh day after leaving Saldang, we crossed Kagmara Pass. Two days later we reached our destination—Rimi, a village ringed by apple orchards.

Renzing's trading partner, Vishnu, greeted him. Renzing and Sonam each hoisted a bag of salt to their shoulders to carry them to Vishnu's house, where the family spends each winter in a single room. The Dolpo-pa walked heavily in their thick woolen boots. Vishnu followed barefooted, his step light and graceful.

Over the next few days, the Dolpo women set up their looms for a winter of weaving blankets to trade in the bazaars of Jumla, and the men settled the yaks on the winter pastures. Then the barter began—Nepalese grain for Tibetan salt from Trabye Tsakha that the Dolpo-pa had acquired in the past summer by trading their barley. In a room of

Vishnu's house Renzing and Vishnu poured salt onto a blanket spread on the floor, one measure of salt for two of grain. With a small copper pot, Renzing scooped salt into a wooden chest. "*Chik, chik, chik*—one, one, one. *Nee, nee, nee*—two, two, two," he counted.

When the salt chests were full, Renzing and Vishnu went to the sunny terrace, where they measured corn and poured it into the salt bags. Children stopped playing to shoo away the chickens that pecked for spilled grain. Sober-faced, the families watched, because the exchange is a trade of life.

Sonam shook the heavy bags to settle the corn, then sewed them shut. Renzing pointed to the bulging bags and exclaimed with a laugh, "They look like full bellies!"

By Diane Summers
Photographs by Eric Valli

In the village of Talphi, Dolpo-pa appraise the bargain that will sustain them another year, if the gods be willing. The amount of Tibetan salt traded for grain grown by the Talphi farmers changes from year to year. The barter may also include manufactured goods from India to be carried home and traded the next year for salt from the other side of the high Himalayan ranges. So the human cycle turns, in tune with its mountain world.

To Fitz Roy's Summit

In October—springtime in Patagonia—my wife, Barbara, and I drove a thousand miles through Argentina to reach a mountain called Fitz Roy near the southern tip of the Andes. With us were Michael Graber and David Wilson, both good friends and veterans of major climbs. Michael, David, and I hoped to scale Fitz Roy, a granite spire named for the captain of the *Beagle,* the ship that in the 1830s carried naturalist Charles Darwin on his epochal voyage around the world.

The mountain's loftiest point rises only 11,073 feet—lower by far than the Himalayan giants or even other Andean summits. But Fitz Roy's sheer walls, combined with unpredictable, raging storms, kept it unclimbed until 1952. In February of that year, two members of a French expedition that included veteran climber Lionel Terray scaled Fitz Roy after a five-week ordeal. One climber died—drowned in a stream on the approach to the mountain. Terray, whose mountaineering exploits included the first ascent of Makalu in the Himalayas, later wrote: "Of all the climbs I have done, the Fitz Roy . . . most nearly approached the limits of my stamina and morale."

Not until 1968 did Americans try Fitz Roy. After waiting out storms for eight weeks, five Californians achieved a fine new route. Their descriptions of the singular beauty of the mountain and its surrounding glaciers and

Mount Fitz Roy's granite spire pierces a passing cloud in Patagonia.

304

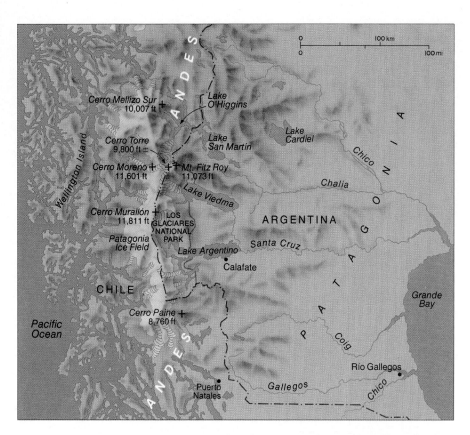

Remote, gripped by glaciers, and battered by gales of the roaring forties dreaded by Cape Horn mariners, Mount Fitz Roy's ice-clad walls present one of the world's most challenging climbs. After its conquest in 1952, Fitz Roy remained unclimbed again for 13 years, when an Argentine expedition reached the summit. It has claimed at least five lives, including two Americans found with ice axes gripped in their frozen hands. The author's party, approaching from the east, relied on speed, skill, and luck to reach the top—on their third attempt. Roped to avoid tumbling into a crevasse, David Wilson (opposite) trudges beneath Fitz Roy's eastern headwall.

ice fields struck a deep chord in me. Fitz Roy beckoned as the ultimate dream climb, but 17 years were to pass before I saw the mountain with my own eyes.

Now, from a campsite 50 miles away, our party first saw Fitz Roy as dawn turned it crimson. Barbara rushed out of the tent with her camera, exclaiming, "It doesn't look real. It's like the shining towers of Oz!"

That otherworldly quality was accentuated by the unfamiliar Patagonian wildlife we had encountered along the way—guanacos, fleet relatives of the camel and llama, and ostrich-like rheas, described by Darwin in 1834.

As we drove the remaining miles westward, Fitz Roy's glaciated bulk rose before us, capped by a monolithic block to rival Yosemite's Half Dome. The road skirted the north edge of Lake Viedma to Los Glaciares National Park in Argentina.

We had arrived at the beginning of a clear spell, the kind of weather some expeditions wait months to enjoy, so we rushed to sign in with park officials and to set up camp at the base of the mountain—a six-mile hike.

Our plan for the climb was to travel light; success would depend on speed and judgment. At the first inkling of bad weather, we would retreat to base camp, rather than hole up on the mountain. If the clear spell lasted, we hoped to climb Fitz Roy in two days. The first day would get us over the glaciered shoulders of the mountain to the upper headwall; the second would be spent climbing 2,200 feet of the headwall, a sheer cliff. Could we do it in a day? David and I had earlier scaled Half Dome's face in one day with plenty of time to spare. But as Mike remarked, "From all I've heard about this mountain, you agree to its terms, not your own."

Morning again; weather clear. We have been climbing several hours now. Barbara remains at base camp. Michael is not with us either. Last night he discovered that his boots were missing and spent the night searching for them. When he didn't return at dawn, David and I split his load and, as agreed, began the climb without him. We have been struggling through deep snow much of the day—burdened by 65-pound packs.

At dusk, just as we climb a final ice gully to a small ledge below the headwall where we intend to bivouac, Michael catches up—a grueling push for him after a sleepless night.

We camp in the open that night, in sleeping bags, and the next morning clouds begin to blow past Fitz Roy at a furious rate. Our sharply edged ridge soon blends into a ground blizzard. We head down.

At the time we had planned to be on top, we reach a frozen lake above base camp. Barbara has hiked there to watch us with binoculars. "I saw you this morning, but I didn't see your camp. Did you spot that yellow tent?"

"What yellow tent?" we ask in unison, totally surprised.

"It's just below the ridge crest. Here, look."

We indeed see a speck of yellow in a cave under a boulder, invisible from the top of the ridge and just minutes away from our route. We continue down to base camp in a thick beech forest near the timberline. Eerie green light seeps through the leaf canopy. The wind, now howling like a turbine on the peaks, barely rustles leaves on the forest floor. Around us stand several crude huts, remnants of earlier expeditions, walled with leaning logs and roofed with plastic tarps— shanties anywhere else, but here they fit with the fantasy of a hobbit world where twisted trees that seem alive climb toward an ultimate mountain.

Two nights after our first attempt the sky clears. Before dawn we are on the mountain, but as we approach the ridge near the headwall, winds are blowing and clouds are moving at tremendous speed. The rope we had cached earlier is missing, blown away by winds that must have exceeded 150 miles per hour. Also gone are a food bag and a bottle of stove fuel. Foiled again. Seventeen hours after we started we are back at our forest home.

Two days later the sky clears and we regain the 6,500 feet to the ridge crest. We find Barbara's yellow dot to be a tarp tied across the entry to a small cave. Its mouth opens onto

a 2,000-foot drop. Behind the tarp, buried in a wall of ice, are the remains of an earlier expedition: ropes, hardware, pots, a stove, a shovel, bags of food. Whoever left them must have been fleeing for their lives.

We christen our cramped chamber the Yellow Submarine. After I crawl into my down sleeping bag, I tie myself to a piton so that I won't slip away in the night. I set my wrist alarm for 3:30, tuck it under my cap next to my ear, and go to sleep under an absolutely clear, still sky.

Sunrise catches Michael working his way up an old, abandoned cable ladder. It lists at a crazy angle out of a vertical sheet of ice, so he attaches his rope to anchors in the rock to protect himself. David then comes up Michael's rope, and I follow with a heavy pack of equipment. I'm halfway up when, suddenly, my foot slips and the rope slides sideways off a bump of ice. I am flung 60 feet through the air in a wild pendulum arc around an overhanging corner. I scream, not because of the swing, but because I see my taut rope dragging across a sharp edge that could sever it.

Everything holds. I am spinning circles in space, 10 feet out from the wall, 2,000 feet above the glacier. Adrenaline surges through my body and my hands begin to shake. I regain my composure—and take photos. Then I finish climbing the rope.

David leads the next section, using both rock- and ice-climbing techniques. He jams one hand into a rock crack; the other hand drives an ax into ice. The going is slow, and by midmorning I feel we can't make it to the top and back down in a day. David and Michael feel the same. Nobody says anything. If we continue, there will be no place to sleep because every ledge is plastered with steeply angled ice. But a look at the sky—cloudless, still, azure—keeps us going.

Late in the afternoon we veer onto a new and untried route. Fitz Roy's long shadow begins to stretch across the valley, and we are in the shade. My fingers stick to metal in the cold. As I lead the way up an overhang, my fingers go numb *(Continued on page 313)*

Storm clouds propelled by heavy winds scud across a ragged skyline dominated by Fitz Roy. Patagonian tempests packing winds of up to 200 miles an hour can blot out the sky in minutes, and demolish ropes, canvas, or any climber caught in the open. The mountain's companion spire, Poincenot Needle, commemorates a French mountaineer lost in 1952. The author's team climbed to the snow-covered notch between the needle and Fitz Roy, then scaled the left flank of its final buttress.

Pages 308-309: Boots fitted with crampons help David Wilson come to grips with an icy toehold en route to a bivouac site during the first assault.

Pages 310-311: Dawn unsheathes the sabertoothed Cerro Torre group west of Fitz Roy. Beyond lie the Patagonian ice field and the snowy peaks of Chile's Cerro Moreno.

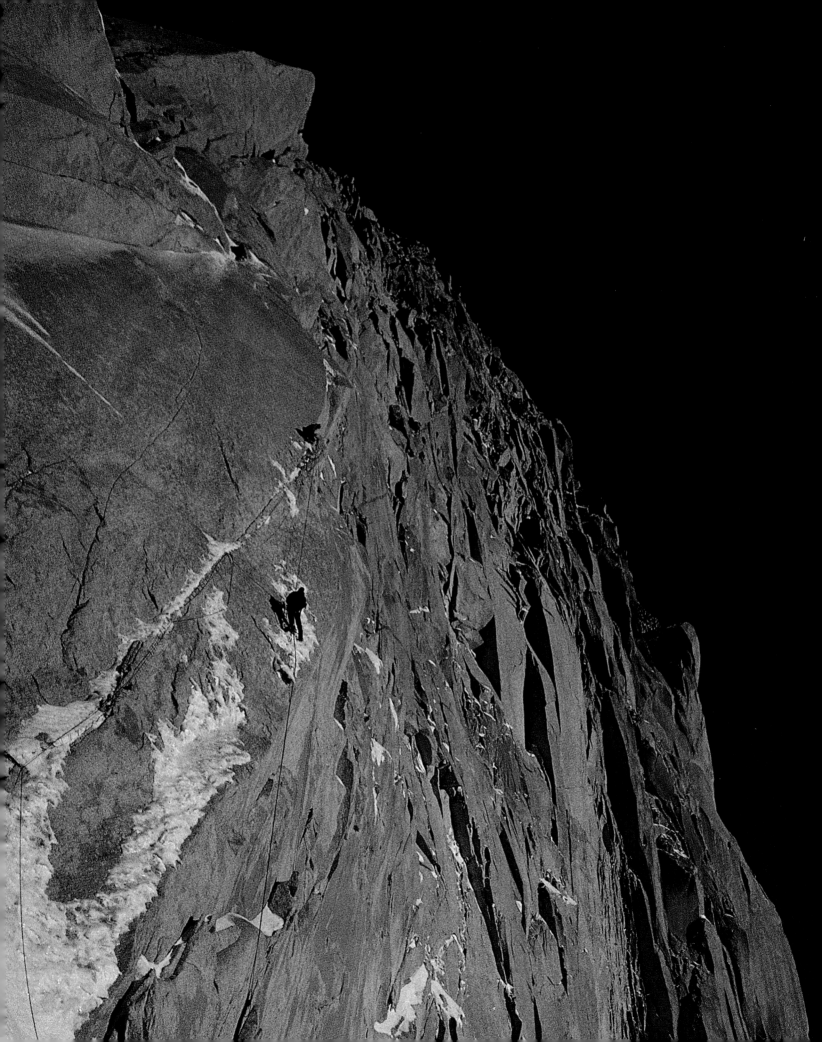

and slip. I fall; the rope stops me after an eight-foot drop. I try again, attach a nylon ladder to my highest anchor, and make it over the lip of the overhang onto the ledge. A sense of well-being flows through me.

Michael leads the next section, then it is my turn again. I can't see beyond the overhangs above me. I try to traverse an icy ledge and can't make it. In growing darkness I climb directly up the overhang and chop ice out of a crack at the lip. Moments later, I stand on a snowfield that slopes toward the summit, just a few hundred feet above. With a sigh of relief I anchor my rope to a rock sticking out of the ice. For the first time today I can stamp out a platform big enough to sit down on. Michael and David find one big enough for two.

We have nothing to look forward to until sunrise, an eternity away. Tonight we will have no sleep, no warmth, no food, no liquid—almost none of the basics needed to sustain existence. We just stand there for seven hours, shuffling, wiggling fingers and toes, sometimes running in place, watching our watches, waiting for the dawn.

When the full moon rises, we join in a

The "Yellow Submarine," a cliffhanging cave shelter abandoned in haste by previous climbers, served the author's group as a precarious overnight perch. Beyond the yellow tarp lies a 2,000-foot drop to the glacier below.

Pitons left by an earlier party and ringlike carabiners strung with fresh webbing provide anchorage for the assault on Fitz Roy's sheer walls.

Inching skyward (opposite) on their final—and successful—attempt to reach the summit, David Wilson ascends a 165-foot rope length anchored from above by Mike Graber. "This is the place I took an unplanned pendulum swing," notes the author, "a little below where David is. I was trying to take out anchors, when my feet slipped on the icy rock. The cliff drops 2,000 vertical feet here. Steep!"

Standing tall—11,073 feet above sea level—as the rising sun throws jagged shadows across the Patagonian ice field, Wilson, Rowell, and Graber experience a moment of triumph "never to be forgotten."

The challenge and reward of their climb are reflected in the words of naturalist John Muir: "Doubly happy . . . is the man to whom lofty mountain tops are within reach, for the lights that shine there illumine all that lies below."

corny rendition of "Harvest Moon" and keep warm to the beat of Michael's imitations of Tina Turner and other rock stars. Our attention turns to the heavens. We recognize only Orion and the Southern Cross. At 3 a.m. a tiny breeze chills us to the core. We can well imagine what a real wind might do.

Dawn brings all the rewards at once. We can see, we can start moving . . . and warm up. The going is easy here, and half an hour later we step onto the summit just after sunrise, as the moon sets over the Patagonian ice field. To the west, two hundred miles of glaciers fill the horizon. To the east, the arid pampas of Argentina stretch as far as our eyes can see. Nearby rise the jagged spires of the Cerro Torre group; and below us shines the great lake, Viedma, fed by an arm of the glacier that calves icebergs into its waters.

The power of the view comes from within us. It would not be the same from an airplane. Michael and David and I, by our own energy, have reached the dominant point on this part of Earth, and we feel a strong connection between what is before our eyes and new knowledge of our inner selves. The minutes we spend on Fitz Roy's crest will become locked in our deepest memory.

Our happiness is restrained. Only when we are safely down the mountain will we celebrate. It takes seven hours and fifteen rappels to bring us back to the safety of the Yellow Submarine, which only yesterday seemed a desperate place. Today it is a palace with everything our hearts desire—warm sleeping bags, hot chocolate, freeze-dried stew, fine company, and sleep.

As we descend the next morning, clouds fill the sky and the wind is blowing again.

By afternoon we reach base camp below the frozen lake. Down where the forest meets the arid plain, berries are beginning to ripen on the calafate bushes. Legend has it that a visitor who tastes this fruit will return to Patagonia. The pungent taste gives me pleasure, something like the land itself.

Text and photographs by Galen Rowell

GOOD BOOKS ABOUT MOUNTAINS

General works: Anthony Huxley's *Standard Encyclopedia of the World's Mountains* (1962) and Edward Pyatt's *The Guinness Book of Mountains and Mountaineering* (1980) contain basic geographic and historical facts arranged for quick reference. Ferdinand Lane introduces the world's mountains and mountain peoples in detail in *The Story of Mountains* (1950).

David Costello discusses the evolution and geology of mountain systems in the United States in *The Mountain World* (1975). *Arctic and Alpine Environments* (1974), edited by Jack D. Ives and Roger G. Barry, is a compendium by an international team of experts.

Scholars and experts present an eloquent "testament to mountain civilization" in *Mountain People* (1986), an anthology edited by Michael Tobias. Larry W. Price demonstrates the variety and fragility of mountain ecosystems worldwide in *Mountains and Man* (1981).

The lure of the high peaks is exuberantly propounded by John Muir in several works, notably *My First Summer in the Sierra* (1911). John Jerome relates geology, geography, literature, and adventure, with a personal touch in *On Mountains* (1978).

Mountains figure as recreation sites in *Backcountry Skiing* (1981) and *Wildwater* (1978), Sierra Club guides by Lito Tejada-Flores. The history of mountaineering unfolds in Ronald Clark's *Men, Myths and Mountains* (1976).

Swiss Alps: *The Transformation of Swiss Mountain Regions* (1984), edited by Ernst Brugger and others, examines ecological, economic, and cultural development. Sir Arnold Lunn covers mountain life and mountaineering in *The Swiss and Their Mountains: A Study of the Influence of Mountains on Man* (1963). *The Playground of Europe* (1871) is by Sir Leslie Stephen, who coined the epithet.

Great Smokies: *A Traveler's Guide to the Smoky Mountains Region* (1985) by Jeff Bradley ranges from Virginia to Georgia. Jerome Doolittle concentrates on natural history in *The Southern Appala-*

chians (1975). Michael Frome's groundbreaking *Strangers in High Places* (1966) tells the story of the establishment of the national park through tales of the people whose lives became entangled with it. Horace Kephart's classic *Our Southern Highlanders* (1913) offers a picture of life among the mountaineers in pre-park days.

Mount Kenya: In *Kenya Mountain* (1929), E.A.T. Dutton recounts his ascent in 1927 with an entourage of porters and English explorers. Iain Allan's *Guide to Mount Kenya and Kilimanjaro* (1981) is a comprehensive handbook for visiting and climbing Africa's two highest mountains.

Denali: In *A Tourist Guide to Mount McKinley* (1974), Bradford Washburn writes about the mountain he mapped. Color pictures highlight flora and fauna in Steve Buskirk's *Denali (Mount McKinley): The Story Behind the Scenery* (1978). Writer John McPhee and photographer Galen Rowell portray the lands and peoples of the "last frontier" in *Alaska: Images of the Country* (1981).

Monteverde: Adrian Forsyth and Kenneth Miyata provide a fascinating introduction to rain forests in *Tropical Nature* (1984). *Costa Rican Natural History* (1983), edited by Daniel Janzen, includes species accounts and checklists of plants and animals. In *A Naturalist in Costa Rica* (1971), Alexander Skutch recalls the adventure of studying forest denizens.

San Juans: Geography professor and former hard-rock miner Thomas Griffiths takes a detailed look at *San Juan Country* (1984). The town of Ouray is the focus of *Mountain Mysteries* (1984) by local historians Marvin Gregory and P. David Smith. *The Rockies* (1968) by David Lavender chronicles the exploration of the U. S. Rockies from the time of the first Europeans to the present.

Mountains of Yunnan: *The Ancient Na-khi Kingdom of Southwest China* (1947, 2 vols.) by explorer-botanist Joseph Rock records the customs of the Naxi, with whom Rock lived for 20 years. C. P.

Fitzgerald presents an account of the lives of the Bai people in *The Tower of Five Glories* (1941).

Tatras: History and geography are emphasized in *The Tatra Mountains* (1942), an interesting profile by Valdemar Firsoff. Irena and Jerzy Kostrowicki present a more recent portrait in the richly illustrated *Poland: Landscape and Architecture* (1980).

Hindu Kush and Karakorams: In *A Short Walk in the Hindu Kush* (1958), Eric Newby regales readers with the trials and tribulations of mountain climbing in Afghanistan, bringing new meaning to the term "culture clash." Geoffrey Moorhouse describes a journey across Pakistan in *To The Frontier* (1984). Biologist George Schaller surveys wildlife and vegetation in *Stones of Silence* (1979).

Tian Shan & Pamirs: Stunning photographs of China's western peaks highlight Galen Rowell's *Mountains of the Middle Kingdom* (1983). The Kazak and Kirgiz tribes are the subject of *High Tartary* (1930) by Owen Lattimore. Morris Rossabi analyzes the region's strategic importance in *China and Inner Asia: From 1368 to the Present Day* (1975).

Pyrenees & Cantabrians: *The Western Pyrenees* (1975) by Daniel Gomez-Ibañez gives a historical view of this French and Spanish borderland. Robert Clark reviews Basque nationalism in *The Basques: The Franco Years and Beyond* (1979) and in his 1984 study, *The Basque Insurgents: ETA, 1952-1980*.

New Guinea Highlands: Exploration from 1875 to the 1960s is the subject of Gavin Souter's *New Guinea: The Last Unknown* (1964). Paula Brown explains the culture, technology, and community life that developed in isolation in *Highland Peoples of New Guinea* (1978). Full of costume and ceremony, *The Highlands of Papua New Guinea* (1983) is a pictorial presentation by Brian Miller.

High Atlas: In *Lords of the Atlas* (1966), Gavin Maxwell relates often grisly tales of the intricate rivalries of the Moroccan Sultanate.

James A. Miller's *Imlil: A Moroccan Mountain Community in Change* (1984) shows Berber adaptation to the modern world. Ernest Gellner's scholarly *Saints of the Atlas* (1969) examines the role of hereditary saints in Berber tribal life.

New Zealand: Peter Radcliffe's *Land of Mountains* (1979) offers a guide to climbing in the islands' beautiful national parks. *High Country* (1980), a photo-essay by Yva Momatiuk and John Eastcott, focuses on the South Island.

Bolivian Andes: Werner Zeil's *The Andes: A Geological Review* (1979) gives information on plate tectonics and mineral deposits. Jeffrey Cole traces the evolution of Indian labor in the mines in his 1985 work, *The Potosí Mita, 1573-1700*. Andean mining towns of the 1930s come to life in the unusual *High Spots in the Andes* (1935), a collection of letters by Josephine Woods, wife of a mining engineer.

Baffin: *The Land That Never Melts: Auyuittuq National Park* explores the geology, archaeology, and natural history of this wilderness. The Royal Society of Canada evaluates economic, social, and political development in *A Century of Canada's Arctic Islands* (1981).

Himalayas: Dazzling peaks, valleys, glaciers, and snowfields fill *Himalayas* (1976), a photographic tour de force by Yoshikazu Shirakawa. In *Everest: A Mountaineering History* (1981) Walt Unsworth gives fascinating details of a hundred years of climbing the world's highest mountain. *Himalayan Pilgrimage* (1961) by David Snellgrove, a Buddhist scholar, describes people and places in northwestern Nepal. *The Snow Leopard* (1978) is Peter Matthiessen's account of an expedition to Dolpo's Shey Mountain to seek the rare feline. *Annapurna: A Woman's Place* (1980) by Arlene Blum is a record of the first women's expedition to the 26,504-foot summit.

Patagonia: Veteran mountaineer Eric Shipton reports his explorations in *Land of Tempest: Travels in Patagonia 1958-1962*, published in 1963. M. A. Azema triumphantly recounts a first ascent in *The Con-*

quest of Fitz Roy (1957). In *Big Wall Climbing* (1974), Doug Scott explains a technical and challenging form of mountaineering and profiles people who pursue it.

In addition, readers may consult the *National Geographic Index* and book lists for many interesting works on mountains of the world.

AUTHORS & PHOTOGRAPHERS

William Albert Allard is a contract photographer with National Geographic. His *American Cowboy* and *Vanishing Breed* reflect his interest in the American West. In the Pyrenees, Allard found that the Basque soul endures in "deep-running traditions."

David Robert Austen is an American photographer who lives in Australia. Photographing New Zealand's mountains, Austen lived on the sheep stations, chopped wood, and hiked the hills with the shepherds of "this beautiful land."

During the last 25 years **Bruno Barbey** has photographed on all continents. His work appears in exhibits and publications worldwide. In shooting the Atlas Mountains, Barbey returned to Morocco, his birthplace.

In the Great Smokies, **James P. Blair** found "an elusive beauty that you have to wait and work for." Blair has been a National Geographic photographer since 1962, and has worked on subjects as varied as coal, astronomy, and Cape Cod, receiving many awards.

Elisabeth B. Booz was born in London, has spent many years in Asia, and lives in France and the United States. She has six books to her credit, including a guide to Tibet and two anthologies of English and American literature for Chinese students.

Douglas H. Chadwick is a writer and wildlife biologist who greets mountain goats and grizzlies not far from the door of his cabin in the Montana Rockies. He views mountains as "crucial strongholds for wildlife across a planet increasingly crowded with people."

Robert P. Clark developed an interest in the culture of the Basque Pyrenees after he married the daughter of an exiled Basque leader. Professor of Government and Politics at George Mason University, Clark has written many works on Basque life and politics.

A National Geographic photographer who grew up in Iran, **Jodi Cobb** has worked worldwide and received many awards. Mountains attract Cobb for their wildness and unpredictability. She was fascinated to see "how the Swiss have tamed their mountains."

Mary B. Dickinson is a National Geographic writer and editor who became familiar with Switzerland in her travels to the source of the Rhône River. For this book, her research took her again to Europe's favorite winter playground.

Ernest B. "Pat" Furgurson, a national columnist and associate editor of the Baltimore *Sun,* has traveled and worked in some 65 countries. He has seen Fuji and the Tian Shan but his heart, says Furgurson, remains in the southern mountains of his youth.

A writer who covers natural history subjects, **Dennis G. Hanson** has climbed and skied in many areas of the world. Hanson participated in the first ascent of a 7,820-foot peak in Antarctica. He lives in Oregon's Cascades.

Photographer **David Hiser** has carried out many mountain-oriented assignments in almost 20 years of shooting for the National Geographic Society. But few, he says, have been as rewarding as the chance to work at home, in the Colorado Rockies.

An anthropologist by training, **Carol Bittig Lutyk** is a National Geographic writer and editor. She has traveled extensively in South America and Europe. With her husband, who once lived in Poland, she explored the Carpathians.

Writer-photographer **Loren McIntyre** has lived and worked in South America most of his life, and has been published in many countries. Of his brush with death on assignment for *Mountain Worlds,* McIntyre said, "I have no desire to ever go down in that mountain again."

George F. Mobley, a National Geographic photographer since 1961, has worked in the mountains of many countries. Mount Kenya was his fifth assignment in Africa, and presented a very different challenge from the rugged, harsh frontier of the Hindu Kush.

Yva Momatiuk and **John Eastcott** are a wife-and-husband team who have photographed and written about many parts of the world. Their National Geographic work has focused on remote areas from New Zealand to the Arctic. Their coverage of the Tatras took them to Poland, Yva's birthplace.

English author **Geoffrey Moorhouse** traveled across Pakistan in order to explore an area whose history was part of his heritage. Moorhouse's much honored books cover many topics, including monasticism, India, cricket, and his 2,000-mile camel trek across the Sahara.

On his world-ranging assignments, photographer **Thomas Nebbia** has made several trips to China. Nebbia says that what he has seen in that rich country is "just the tip of the iceberg." Nebbia's work appears in leading publications and museum exhibits.

Elizabeth L. Newhouse grew up in Latin America. A former Peace Corps member, she has worked as a National Geographic staffer on a dozen books. On assignment for this book, she discovered a spiritual power permeating the world of the Atlas Mountains.

Robert M. Poole, raised in the foothills of North Carolina's Blue Ridge, now lives within sight of the Virginia Blue Ridge. An editor and writer for the Geographic, Poole has visited China on assignment three times in recent years.

A former Navy pilot, **David F. Robinson** has been a National Geographic writer and editor for 22 years, and a mountain hiker all his life. Author of two books and many articles on nature, he was amazed by the exuberant variety of life on Monteverde's clouded ridge.

Galen Rowell combined three passions—mountain climbing, photography, and writing—to document his ascent of Mount Fitz Roy. Rowell's books and articles depict mountain life and adventure in California, Alaska, China, India, Pakistan, and Nepal.

An Australian lawyer, **Diane Summers** found a new career as a writer when she began to live and travel with people of the Himalayas. With photographer Eric Valli, she explores the relationships between the people and the mountains.

Lito Tejada-Flores suggests that his birth in the Bolivian Andes at an altitude of 13,000 feet may explain his love for mountain life today. Tejada-Flores is a filmmaker, skier, and writer who lives in the Colorado Rockies.

The photographs of **William E. Thompson** appear in national magazines. Thompson found a stern test in the steady month-long rain and knee-deep mud of his mountaintop assignment in Costa Rica. He counts his recent flights around Mount Everest to be true adventure.

A free-lance travel and science writer before joining National Geographic, **Jonathan B. Tourtellot** has walked and talked his way up mountains in places as diverse as Tanzania, Peru, Colorado, England, and Iceland.

Eric Valli, born in France, is a former cabinetmaker who became a photographer when he fell in love with Nepal. Valli lives in Kathmandu. He works with Diane Summers to document Himalayan life for international publishers.

ACKNOWLEDGMENTS

318

We thank the persons and organizations named or quoted in *Mountain Worlds*. In addition, we are grateful to the following for their generous help in the preparation of this book: Mohammad Akram, Nigel Allan, Manuel Aramayo, Peter Bakewell, Joseph W. Bastien, Deborah Bell, Daryl J. Boness, James E. Bosson, Ray Breneman, Laurie Chamberlain, Chen Yongling, Marie Clark, Jonathan A. Coddington, Phillip Cribb, Doug Cuillard, David Deal, Craig d'Entremont, Gary Diller, William A. Douglass, Theodore R. Dudley, Paul A. Dunn, Jamila Elhilali, Robert B. Faden, Juan Fernandez, Elizabeth W. Fernea, Dori Florin, Bill Greenwood, Ruth and Marvin Gregory, Kenn Harper, Dana Isherwood, Jack D. Ives, Corneille Jest, Schuyler Jones, Roy Juvet, Abdulla Kadir, Fred Kaufman, Kim Ho-Dong, Elżbieta Kotarska, Hanni Kunz, Peter Kuntze, Cynthia Gravelle LeCount, David B. Lellinger, Li Jianping, Thomas E. Lovejoy, Mark McCann, Mumtaz Malik, Mervyn Meggitt, Paul Messerli, James A. Miller, Peter Molnar, J. R. Morton, Leslie and Ruedi Mullener, Murad Khan Nayyar, Miriam Rovsing Olsen, Leo Orleans, Robert Orndruff, Wilson Mendieta Pacheco, Robert E. Padden, Burton Pu, Peter H. Raven, Emile Raynaud, Heinz Rufer, Will Russell, George B. Schaller, Christopher R. Scotese, Shen Shoujun, Richard F. Strand, Su Wancheng, Georges Tauxe, Jean-Claude Thomas, Ron Warfield, Werner Wieser, Manfred Wolf, Robin D. S. Yates, Yu Zhengwen, Abdul-Rauf Yousaf Zai, Elsa Zardini; and the National Geographic Society Library, Illustrations Library, Administrative Services, Translations Division, and Travel Office.

INDEX

Type composition by National Geographic's Photographic Services. Color separations by Chanticleer Co., Inc., New York, N.Y.; Dai Nippon Printing Company Ltd, Tokyo, Japan; The Lanman Companies, Washington, D. C.; Litho Studios Ltd, Dublin, Ireland. Printed and bound by R. R. Donnelley & Sons Co., Chicago, Ill. Paper by Mead Paper Co., New York, N.Y.

Library of Congress CIP Data:

Mountain worlds.

Bibliography: p.
Includes index.
1. Mountains. 2. Mountain life. I. National Geographic Book Service.
GB511.M68 1988   508.314'3   86-16472
ISBN 0-87044-651-7 (alk. paper)
ISBN 0-87044-652-5 (lib. bdg. : alk. paper)
ISBN 0-87044-653-3 (deluxe : alk. paper)